P · O · C · K · E · T · S

SHARKS

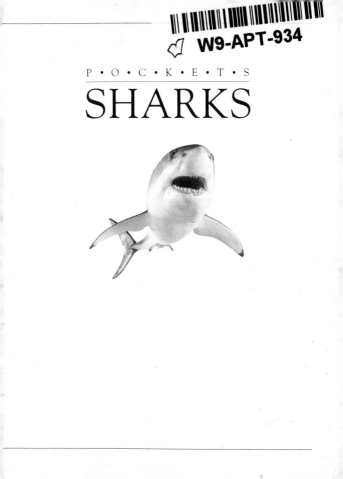

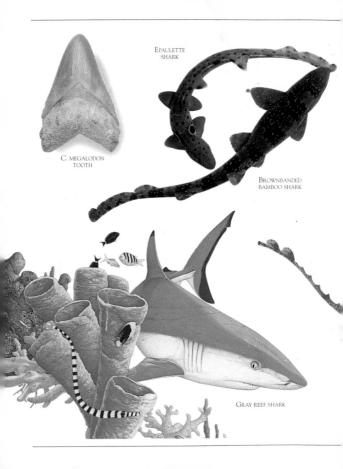

C. MEGALODON
TOOTH

EPAULETTE
SHARK

BROWNBANDED
BAMBOO SHARK

GRAY REEF SHARK

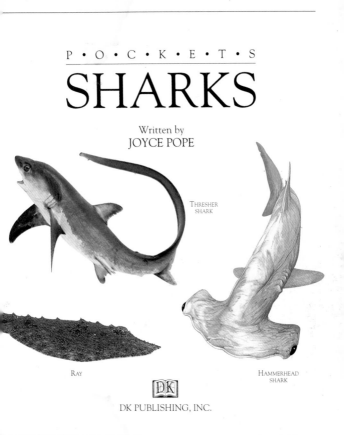

P · O · C · K · E · T · S

SHARKS

Written by
JOYCE POPE

THRESHER
SHARK

RAY

HAMMERHEAD
SHARK

DK
DK PUBLISHING, INC.

A DK PUBLISHING BOOK

Project editor	Anna McMurray
Art editors	Martin Wilson
	Jacqui Burton
Design assistant	Tanya Tween
Senior editor	Alastair Dougall
Senior art editors	Carole Oliver
	Sarah Crouch
Picture research	Neil Aldridge
Production	Kate Oliver
US Editor	Irene Pavitt

First American edition, 1997
2 4 6 8 10 9 7 5 3 1
Published in the United States by
DK Publishing, Inc., 95 Madison Avenue
New York, New York 10016

Copyright © 1997 Dorling Kindersley Ltd.

Visit us on the World Wide Web at
http://www.dk.com

Published in Great Britain by Dorling Kindersley Ltd.

A catalog record is available from
the Library of Congress.

ISBN 0-7894-2045-7

Color reproduction by Colourscan, Singapore
Printed and bound in Italy by L.E.G.O.

CONTENTS

HOW TO USE THIS BOOK

These pages show you how to use *Pockets: Sharks*. The book is divided into five sections. The first four provide information about the anatomy, behavior, and the different species of sharks. The last section contains a classification table, followed by a glossary and a comprehensive index.

ALL ABOUT SHARKS
This book has been divided into five sections. Turn to the contents pages, index, or glossary for more information about anatomy, types of species, behavior, or the role of sharks in science and conservation.

CORNER CODING
The corners of the main section pages are color coded to remind you which section you are in.

 ANATOMY

 LIVING AND SURVIVING

SHARKS AND HUMANS

 SHARK DIRECTORY

SHARKS FOR THE FUTURE

HEADING
The heading describes the subject of the page. This page is about the feeding habits and tooth shapes of various sharks.

INTRODUCTION
The introduction provides an overview of the subject. After reading this, you should have a clear idea of what the pages are about.

Corner coding

Heading

Introduction

LIVING AND SURVIVING

FEEDING HABITS

SHARKS EAT MANY different types of food, but all are flesh-eaters. Most eat small fish or invertebrates and some will grab carrion when they can. Three large species filter food, known as plankton, from the sea. Some sharks hunt large animals, including sea lions and other sharks.

GENTLE EAT
The whale shark eats food only on plankton. Mobilike long tiny crustations from the water passes over its gills. On occasion the whale shark has an active hunter, preying on shoals of small fish, such as anchovy.

FEEDING FACTS
• Sharks do not need to feed every day.
• Undigested food may remain in the stomach for several days.
• Smell and the lateral line are the principal senses used by the shark to lead it to food.

SHARP TEETH
The horn shark uses its some of small to locate animals such as sea urchins and shellfish, on which it feeds. They are caught with its sharp front teeth and crushed with flat teeth in the back of its mouth.

Fact box   *Annotation*

LABELS
For extra clarity, some pictures have labels. A label identifies a picture if it is not immediately obvious what it is from the text.

These remind you which section you are in.
The top of the left-hand page gives the
section name, and the top of the right-
hand page gives the subject heading. The
page on feeding habits is from the Living
and Surviving section.

FACT BOXES
Many pages have fact boxes. These
provide at-a-glance information
about a subject, such as how long
undigested food can remain in the
stomach, and what senses the shark

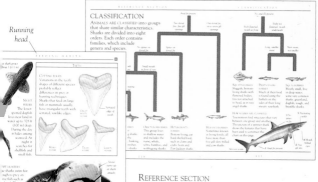

*Running
head*

CLASSIFICATION
ANIMALS ARE CLASSIFIED into groups
that share similar characteristics.
Sharks are divided into eight
orders. Each order contains
families, which include
genera and species.

FEEDING HABITS

TEETH

CUTTING TEETH
Variations in the teeth
shapes of different species
probably reflect
differences in prey or
hunting techniques.
Sharks that feed on large
fish or mammals usually
have triangular teeth with
serrated, sawlike edges.

Caption   Label

CAPTIONS AND ANNOTATIONS
Each illustration carries an
explanatory caption. Some also
have annotations, in *italics*.
These point out the features of
an illustration, and often use
leader lines.

REFERENCE SECTION
The reference pages are yellow and appear at
the back of the book. On these, you will find a
classification table, and other interesting facts
and records about sharks. There is a list of
conservation organizations and aquariums on
the resources pages.

INDEX
At the back of the book is an index listing
every subject in the book. By referring to
the index, information on particular topics
can be found quickly. A glossary defines the
technical terms used in the book.

INTRODUCTION

ABOUT SHARKS

SHARKS ROAM all the oceans of the world. Most are large, and all are flesh-eaters. Your first sight may be a dark, triangular fin moving steadily through the water. Closer in, you will see the series of gill slits behind the head and the pointed snout that overhangs the mouth.

HAMMERHEAD
Sharks are generally solitary creatures, but sharks such as green dogfish, blue sharks, and some kinds of hammerhead shark swim in groups.

The great white is the only shark able to lift its head out of the water to inspect surface objects

Pointed snout

Light-colored underbelly

GREAT WHITE
There are more than 340 species of sharks. The most feared is the great white or white pointer, which lives near the surface of tropical seas. Its main food is large fish, turtles, and seals. It is big enough to regard human beings as prey, and it has been responsible for many attacks on people.

Pectoral fin

ONE-YEAR-OLD
LEOPARD SHARK

SHARK SPOTS

The leopard shark gets its name from its spotted skin. Its teeth have rounded tops for crushing the hard-shelled creatures, such as clams and sea snails, on which it feeds. This shark is frequently kept in marine aquariums since it adapts well to captivity.

*This shark is
15 in (38 cm)
in length*

HORN SHARK

The horn shark is a slow, bottom-living species. It feeds on hard-shelled prey and is harmless unless disturbed. It lays eggs in spiral-shaped egg cases, which it wedges into crevices in rocks to keep them safe from enemies until they hatch.

*Spotted pattern
on skin*

Pelvic fin

SHARK EATS MUM ALIVE AS KIDS WATCH

Horror on dive at nature spot

A MOTHER of five was bitten in two by a 13ft shark while her children watched in horror from a boat.

NEWS SENSATION

A human stands little chance in an encounter with a large shark, as this attack in Australia demonstrates. Shark attacks always make the headlines. They often take place close to land in shallow water, where children play and most people swim.

THE SHARK'S DOMAIN

THE WORLD'S OCEANS are the shark's domain.
A few species, such as the blue shark, are found
throughout the warmer parts of this vast area, but
many are restricted to certain coasts or to types of
watery habitat, such as muddy bays or the edges of
coral reefs. The majority live in the well-lit surface
zone, but a few are only found in very deep water.

SEA HOME
Nurse sharks are often found where the sea is
shallow. On the outer side of a reef, where the
water is deeper, species such as the blacktip reef
shark abound. The blue shark and the
great white, both fast-swimming
hunters, and the slow-moving,
huge whale shark are most
often seen in the open seas.
The strange-looking lantern
and goblin shark live in the
depths of the ocean.

Continental shelf

Continental slope

Blacktip reef shark

FRESHWATER EXPLORERS
Bull sharks inhabit
tropical rivers and
lakes as well as the
sea. They have
been spotted 2,298
miles (3,700 km) from
the sea in the Amazon River.
They are a great danger to
other river dwellers.

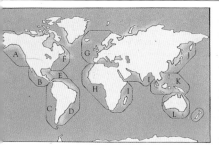

WORLD MAP
This map shows the distribution of coastal-living sharks. Some, such as the whale shark, may live in many places, while the green dogfish is known from only one area. Some oceanic sharks may venture into inshore waters but do not stay there long.

A. WESTERN NORTH AMERICA: Horn shark
B. WESTERN CENTRAL AMERICA: Bull shark
C. WESTERN SOUTH AMERICA: Swell shark
D. EASTERN SOUTH AMERICA: Cookiecutter shark
E. WEST INDIES: Green dogfish
F. EASTERN NORTH AMERICA: Greenland shark

G. WESTERN EUROPE: Porbeagle
H. WEST AFRICA: Gulper shark
I. E. AFRICA, S. ASIA: Blacktip reef shark
J. NORTHEASTERN ASIA: Goblin shark
K. POLYNESIA: Whale shark
L. AUSTRALIA: Wobbegong

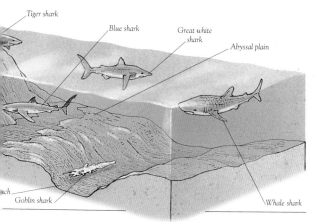

Tiger shark

Blue shark

Great white shark

Abyssal plain

Goblin shark

Whale shark

EARLY EVIDENCE

THE TEETH of sharks are common fossils. The first sharks lived about 380 million years ago, in a sea that covered what is now Ohio. When they died, they sank so quickly into the silt on the seabed that their skeletons are well preserved.

SPIRAL FOSSIL TEETH
Unlike other sharks, *Helicoprion* retained its teeth in its upper and lower jaws rather than shedding them at regular intervals. The oldest teeth are in the middle of the spiral.

Diameter of teeth whorl is about 6.5 in (17 cm)

Teeth were constantly pushed back, forming a spiral

HELICOPRION
Scientists are unsure exactly what *Helicoprion* looked like, or fed on, since only its teeth have ever been found. This shark survived for nearly 100 million years but left no descendants. Its fossils are widespread throughout the world.

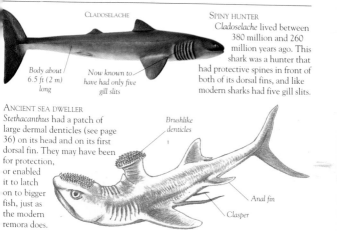

CLADOSELACHE

Body about 6.5 ft (2 m) long

Now known to have had only five gill slits

SPINY HUNTER
Cladoselache lived between 380 million and 260 million years ago. This shark was a hunter that had protective spines in front of both of its dorsal fins, and like modern sharks had five gill slits.

ANCIENT SEA DWELLER
Stethacanthus had a patch of large dermal denticles (see page 36) on its head and on its first dorsal fin. They may have been for protection, or enabled it to latch on to bigger fish, just as the modern remora does.

Brushlike denticles

Anal fin

Clasper

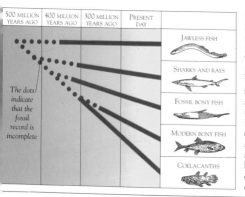

500 MILLION YEARS AGO	400 MILLION YEARS AGO	300 MILLION YEARS AGO	PRESENT DAY	
				JAWLESS FISH
				SHARKS AND RAYS
				FOSSIL BONY FISH
				MODERN BONY FISH
				COELACANTHS

The dots indicate that the fossil record is incomplete

FISH EVOLUTION
Fish have lived in the sea for nearly 500 million years. The first fish were jawless, like lampreys. Modern fish appeared at the end of the Age of Dionosaurs, about 65 million years ago. *Coelacanth* and sturgeons have survived the extinction of most of their relatives.

ANCIENT SHARKS

SINCE THE FIRST SHARKS evolved, ways of life in the sea have changed very little. As a result, many of today's sharks are much like their ancient ancestors – some are so similar that people think of them as living fossils. As such they can tell us a great deal about animals that may have been extinct for many millions of years.

PORT JACKSON SHARK

OLD RELATIVES
Fossils of fish very similar to the Port Jackson shark have been found in rocks 150 million years old. They fed on hard-shelled prey such as oysters and clams, which they crushed with strangely shaped, ridged teeth

ELUSIVE SPECIES
The frilled shark lives in deeper water than many other species and remained unknown to science until the late 19th century. Unusual-looking on the outside, it is even stranger under the skin, for some parts of its skeleton resemble those of sharks that became extinct 350 million years ago.

FRILLED SHARK

Eel-shaped body

MONSTER MOUTH
The biggest shark teeth ever found belong to a fossil that lived about 60 million years ago. It is possible that *Carcharodon meglodon* grew to a length of over 54.5 ft (16.6 m) and weighed about 22 tons (20 tonnes).

Some people believe Meglodon may still exist in deep water

GREAT WHITE TOOTH

C. MEGLODON TOOTH

LARGER THAN LIFE
This illustration is less than life size, for the actual-sized tooth would be taller than this page! Teeth from sharks this big have been dredged from the seabed and estimated to be about 11,000 years old.

Both teeth are 75 percent of their actual size

SLOW GOING
Hybodus was the most common shark during the time of the dinosaurs. The shape of its tail suggests that it was not a fast swimmer.

Spine on second dorsal fin

Long upper lobe

CLOSE RELATIVES

IT IS HARD TO BELIEVE that flat, slow-moving skates and rays, which live on the bed of the sea, are related to fast, streamlined sharks. However, rays' and sharks' anatomy is very similar: for example, both have cartilaginous skeletons (see page 34) and up to seven gill slits.

Underside is pale in color, while upper surface is camouflaged

SEABED FEEDER
Rays feed mainly on sand-living creatures, so their mouths are on the underside of their bodies. There is a hole called a spiracle on the upper side, through which clean water for breathing is taken in and passed over the gills.

MOLLUSKS
Rays feed on hard-shelled animals, such as sea snails, that live in the sand.

Grinding teeth crush the armour of prey

POISON GLAND
Some rays have sharp, saw-like stings on their tails. These are good protection against their enemies.

Winglike fins

MANTA
RAY

FLIPPER FEEDING
Manta rays have forsaken the bottom-living habits of
other rays and swim in surface waters, using their great
fins like slow-moving wings. These huge fish feed on
plankton, which they guide into their mouths with
flipperlike organs on either side of their heads.

*Flippers for
guiding food*

SUN BATHER
The pygmy devil ray is smaller than
the great manta. In warm seas, it can
sometimes be seen lying on the surface,
before leaping out of the water
and speeding away.

MOBULA
WITH
REMORAS

*Remoras hitching
a ride*

FLOATING FOOD
Plankton is largely made up
of tiny marine plants and
animals that float at the
mercy of the currents.
This nutritious "soup"
drifts on or near the
surface of the sea.

ANATOMY

NOSE TO TAIL

MOST SHARKS are large fish, designed for constant, effortless swimming, though not at sustained high speeds. Their color is usually a bluish gray, to blend with the colors of the ocean. Their senses, like their teeth, are razor-sharp, and they are quick to investigate anything that could be food.

Long gill slits

Near-symmetrical long upper and lower caudal (tail) lobes

Swimming keel

Pelvic fin

HARMLESS FISH
The largest fish in the world is the whale shark which can reach 43 ft (13 m) long and weigh 24 tons (22 tonnes). Like the largest of the whales, these fish feed on very small organisms that they strain from the sea.

This drawing of a person to scale gives an idea of the whale shark's large size

Nostril

Upturned snout

DIFFERENT SHAPES AND SIZES

The prickly dogfish has a very high dorsal fin on its body. Hammerhead sharks carry their eyes and nostrils on the outside of their wide head. Sharks such as the wobbegong and the angel shark are well camouflaged to blend in with their surroundings on the seabed.

Sharp, serrated teeth

Pectoral fin

GREAT FISH

As the great white swims, it steers and balances itself with its stiff fins. Its upturned snout is counterbalanced by the long upper lobe of the tail. Like most sharks, it is a solitary hunter, though if there is a glut of food a number may gather to feed.

HAMMERHEAD

PRICKLY DOGFISH

SPOTTED WOBBEGONG

TAILS AND FINS

A SHARK PROPELS itself through the water by moving
its powerful tail from side to side. Unlike most fish,
a shark's fins are supported internally by rods of
cartilage. They cannot be folded against its body but
project outward, controlling the direction of the shark
and acting as a braking mechanism.

SWIMMING AID
The shape of a shark's tail is
important to the speed it
can swim. Sharks with
evenly balanced caudal fins
(tails) are the fastest
swimmers, whereas slower
sharks may have hardly any
lower lobe to their tail.

*Enlarged upper
caudal lobe*

THRASHING TAIL
A thresher shark uses its tail to
help it get food. Beating the water with the
long upper lobe of its tail frightens and stuns
small fish, making them easier to catch.

FAST-MOVING
Each stroke of the
tail tends to drive
the great white
downward, since the
upper lobe is slightly
longer. However, water
movement around the
upturned snout
keeps the shark
balanced.

Dorsal fin

*Symmetrical tail has
evolved for slow and
fast swimming*

Pectoral fin

UNIQUE TAIL
Angel sharks have very large fins, which make them look like skates. Like skates, they live on the seabed, but they swim like sharks, using their slender tails and not their fins for propulsion. Unlike most sharks, the lower lobe of an angel shark's tail is bigger than the upper lobe.

SHAPELY TAIL
The swell shark, which lives in kelp beds close to the shore, has a tail that is not designed for fast swimming. In spite of this, the swell shark is a very effective hunter of small fish.

Second dorsal fin

TAIL OF SWELL SHARK

SEABED DWELLER
The horn shark has large fins and a small tail for its size. Tagging has shown that it sometimes swims long distances from its breeding areas.

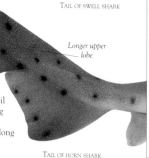

Longer upper lobe

TAIL OF HORN SHARK

FIN FACTS

• Sharks steer using their paired (pectoral and pelvic) fins which function like the wings of an aircraft.

• The horny rods of shark fins are cut off and dried to make soup.

• The inner edge of the male's pelvic fins forms a pair of mating organs called claspers.

INSIDE THE BODY

IMMEDIATELY BENEATH the skin of a shark lie the zigzag muscles that swing the body from side to side as it swims. In the body cavity below is the heart and digestive system. The intestine is fairly straight, apart from the spiral valve, which adds to the area in which digested food can be absorbed. Contrary to popular belief, sharks are not stupid animals and have a larger brain for their body size than most bony fish.

Dorsal fin

Segmented swimming muscles

Spiral valve

Rectal gland

First dorsal fin

Pancreas

Spleen, produces red blood cells

BODY FACTS

• Large olfactory lobes in the brain show how important the sense of smell is to a shark.

• The tongue is supported by a pad of cartilage.

• The gallbladder releases a greenish fluid called bile into the gut; it aids digestion.

HEART OF A SHARK

Sharks have a four-chambered heart that lies forward, close to the gills. Blood returning from the body loaded with carbon dioxide enters the rear chamber and is pumped forward to the gills, where it is released. A new supply of oxygen is then taken up and the cycle is repeated.

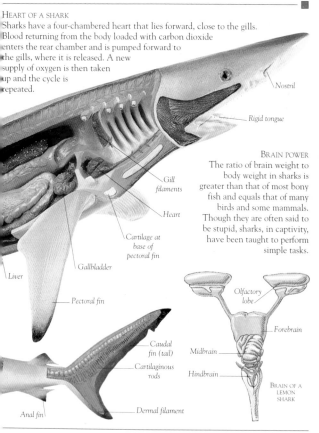

Nostril

Rigid tongue

Gill filaments

Heart

Cartilage at base of pectoral fin

Gallbladder

Liver

Pectoral fin

Caudal fin (tail)

Cartilaginous rods

Anal fin

Dermal filament

BRAIN POWER

The ratio of brain weight to body weight in sharks is greater than that of most bony fish and equals that of many birds and some mammals. Though they are often said to be stupid, sharks, in captivity, have been taught to perform simple tasks.

Olfactory lobe

Forebrain

Midbrain

Hindbrain

BRAIN OF A LEMON SHARK

Gills and liver

A shark breathes by taking water into its mouth and pumping it over the gills that lie behind its head. As the water flows past, oxygen in it is removed and passes into the bloodstream to be used in the shark's body. The liver contains high quantities of oil that aid buoyancy – like the swim bladder of a bony fish.

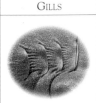

SHUT
As the shark takes water into its mouth (the equivalent of breathing in), the gill slits are closed.

OPEN
Water and carbon dioxide waste are expelled when the gill slits are open.

EATING AND BREATHING
Basking sharks use their gill slits for feeding as well as breathing. Attached to the gill supports are comblike structures called gill rakers that filter plankton from seawater.

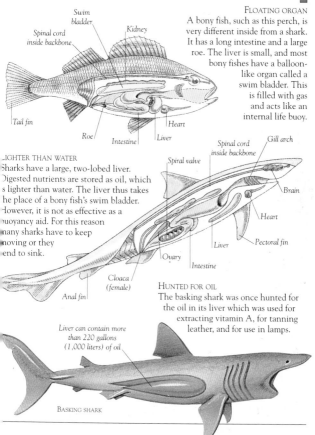

Swim
bladder

Spinal cord
inside backbone

Kidney

FLOATING ORGAN

A bony fish, such as this perch, is
very different inside from a shark.
It has a long intestine and a large
roe. The liver is small, and most
bony fishes have a balloon-
like organ called a
swim bladder. This
is filled with gas
and acts like an
internal life buoy.

Tail fin

Roe

Intestine

Heart

Liver

LIGHTER THAN WATER

Sharks have a large, two-lobed liver.
Digested nutrients are stored as oil, which
is lighter than water. The liver thus takes
the place of a bony fish's swim bladder.
However, it is not as effective as a
buoyancy aid. For this reason
many sharks have to keep
moving or they
tend to sink.

Spiral valve

Spinal cord
inside backbone

Gill arch

Brain

Heart

Liver

Pectoral fin

Ovary

Intestine

Cloaca
(female)

Anal fin

HUNTED FOR OIL

The basking shark was once hunted for
the oil in its liver which was used for
extracting vitamin A, for tanning
leather, and for use in lamps.

Liver can contain more
than 220 gallons
(1,000 liters) of oil

BASKING SHARK

JAWS AND TEETH

SHARKS HAVE UPPER AND LOWER jaws, but, unlike most other animals with backbones, their jaws are only loosely attached to the skull. When a shark bites its prey, the jaws are forced forward, allowing the teeth to be used more efficiently.

DOGFISH

PORT JACKSON

Living sharks cannot open their jaws as wide as this

Small teeth are used for catching bottom-living fish and crabs

These teeth are used for grabbing and crunching its prey

RENEWABLE TEETH
Shark teeth are arranged in rows. There are usually six or more rows of replacement teeth constantly developing in the mouth. The teeth in the front row slash at prey. As soon as one becomes slightly blunted or damaged, it falls out and another tooth from behind slips into place

The tiger shark has strong teeth capable of crunching through a turtle's bones and shell

TIGER SHARK JAWS

Tiny teeth not used for feeding

SANDPAPER TEETH
Basking sharks do not tear or crush their food, so their teeth are small, resembling coarse sandpaper.

CRUSHING TEETH

Port Jackson sharks feed on hard-shelled animals without backbones, such as crabs and sea urchins. A pad of small, sharp teeth in the front of their mouths seizes the prey from the seabed. In the back of the jaws is a battery of flat, pebblelike teeth that crushes the armor of their victims.

SECTION THROUGH A PORT JACKSON'S JAWS

BITE-SIZE HOLES

The cookiecutter shark is named after the circular chunks of flesh it bites from its prey. It has small, sharp teeth and feeds on big fish, whales, and seals, all much larger than itself. Cookiecutters shed an entire row of teeth at one time, usually swallowing them with their food.

Cookiecutter's lips cling onto prey like suckers

HUNGRY TEETH

The sand tiger raises its overhanging snout as it attacks its prey. Its pointed teeth are ideal for grabbing and holding fish. It has a huge appetite and may eat more than 99 lb (45 kg) of food in a single meal.

SKELETONS

SHARKS ARE DIFFERENT from all other animals and humans in that their skeletons contain no bone. Instead, they are made from a soft, flexible, gristly material called cartilage. In some sharks, part of the skeleton is strengthened with calcium salts, particularly in the bones of the back, jaws, and braincase.

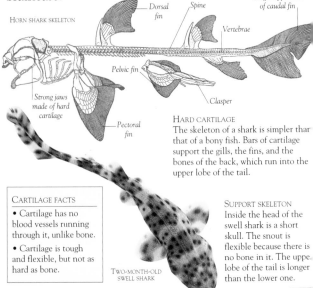

HORN SHARK SKELETON

Dorsal fin

Spine

Vertebrae

Longer upper lobe of caudal fin

Strong jaws made of hard cartilage

Pelvic fin

Pectoral fin

Clasper

TWO-MONTH-OLD SWELL SHARK

HARD CARTILAGE
The skeleton of a shark is simpler than that of a bony fish. Bars of cartilage support the gills, the fins, and the bones of the back, which run into the upper lobe of the tail.

SUPPORT SKELETON
Inside the head of the swell shark is a short skull. The snout is flexible because there is no bone in it. The upper lobe of the tail is longer than the lower one.

CARTILAGE FACTS
• Cartilage has no blood vessels running through it, unlike bone.
• Cartilage is tough and flexible, but not as hard as bone.

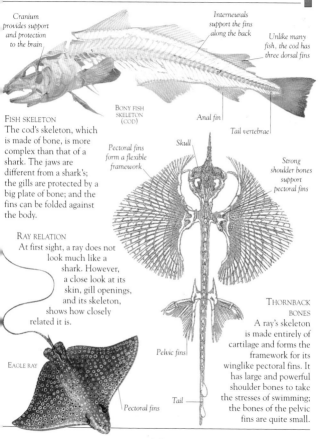

Cranium provides support and protection to the brain

Interneurals support the fins along the back

Unlike many fish, the cod has three dorsal fins

BONY FISH SKELETON (COD)

Anal fin

Tail vertebrae

FISH SKELETON

The cod's skeleton, which is made of bone, is more complex than that of a shark. The jaws are different from a shark's; the gills are protected by a big plate of bone; and the fins can be folded against the body.

Pectoral fins form a flexible framework

Skull

Strong shoulder bones support pectoral fins

RAY RELATION

At first sight, a ray does not look much like a shark. However, a close look at its skin, gill openings, and its skeleton, shows how closely related it is.

EAGLE RAY

Pelvic fins

Pectoral fins

Tail

THORNBACK BONES

A ray's skeleton is made entirely of cartilage and forms the framework for its winglike pectoral fins. It has large and powerful shoulder bones to take the stresses of swimming; the bones of the pelvic fins are quite small.

SKIN

A SHARK'S SKIN is protected, not by scales, but by small, hard "skin teeth" or dermal denticles. Denticles vary in shape from one part of the body to another. They are rounded on its snout and pointed on its back; in the jaws, the denticles develop into powerful teeth.

19th-century samurai sword

DENTICLES
x 10 MAGNIFICATION

SKIN TEETH
A shark's dermal denticles are covered with enamel. Below the enamel is a layer of dentine, which is the basic material of most teeth. Each dentine layer has a cavity which has a bony base, containing blood vessels and nerves, set deep in the skin.

HARDWEARING DECORATION
The skin of many sharks is used for making leather or a natural type of sandpaper called shagreen. This Japanese samurai sword is enclosed in a sheath of ray skin. The skin has been polished and lacquered so that its denticles are smooth.

SKIN DETAIL OF LESSER-SPOTTED DOGFISH

It is possible to see growth rings on the scale of a fish which indicate its age

FISH SCALE

BRAMBLE SHARK SKIN

A few kinds of shark have very small denticles or even smooth skin. A bramble shark has scattered denticles, some of which have a tuft of little spikes like the thorns of a blackberry.

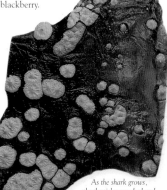

SCALE BONES
The scales of a bony fish, such as a salmon or perch, are made of thin slips of bone, set in the skin like the overlapping tiles on a roof. As the fish grows, the scales increase in size.

As the shark grows, the denticles are shed and replaced by larger ones

WELL DISGUISED
The wobbegong matches the color of the seabed on which it lies. Its prey is lured by the fringe of tassels around its mouth. The wobbegong's mouth looks like seaweed to the creatures it eats.

LIVING AND SURVIVING

SENSES

A SHARK'S SENSES tell it about the world in which it lives. Besides being able to see, smell, and hear, a shark can also sense movements and electrical fields made by other animals in the water. Using this sense of "touch," it locates food or enemies. The sharpness of a shark's senses varies from one species to another depending on lifestyle.

ELECTRICAL SENSITIVITY
On the head of a shark are small, dark pores named the ampullae of Lorenzini. These openings connect to organs that detect faint electrical signals generated by the muscle activity of a shark's prey.

Nostril

Eye

Ampullae of Lorenzini

SANDTIGER SHARK

LATERAL LINE
Down each side of its body and up to its head, a shark has a series of pressure-sensitive organs called its lateral line. Tiny changes in water pressure caused by other fish can be detected – highly useful in darkness or murky water.

Lateral line

BALANCE MECHANISM
When a shark turns or changes level, liquid moves against the hairlike organs that line the canals of the ear. Ear stones move as the shark changes speed, keeping it informed of position and movement.

Large nostrils of horn shark

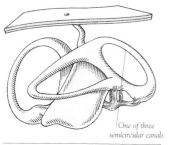

One of three semicircular canals

SCENT DETECTORS
As a shark swims, water constantly flows into its nostril sacs, which are lined with scent-detecting cells.

EYES

Sharks can see well in dim light. Their eyes have a layer of cells called a tapetum that reflects light back onto the retina. In bright light they can close the pupil to a narrow slit. Some sharks have a light-blocking screen to filter light.

DOGFISH WITH CLOSED PUPIL

HORN SHARK'S PUPIL

RAY EYE WITH SCREEN

Barbels

FOOD FEELERS
Nurse sharks feed mostly on animals without backbones. Fleshy, finger-like barbels at the front of the mouth probe the sand of the seabed for food, perhaps also gathering information about the smell and taste of the prey.

FEEDING HABITS

SHARKS EAT MANY different types of food, but all are flesh-eaters. Most eat small fish or invertebrates and some will grab carrion when they can. Three large species filter food, known as plankton, from the sea. Some sharks hunt large animals, including sea lions and other sharks.

GENTLE EATER
The whale shark mainly feeds on plankton. Meshlike filters sift tiny creatures from the water that passes over its gills. On occasion the whale shark becomes an active hunter, preying on shoals of small fish, such as anchovy.

FEEDING FACTS
• Sharks do not need to feed every day.
• Undigested food may remain in the stomach for several days.
• Smell and the lateral line are the principal senses used by the shark to lead it to food.

SHARP TEETH
The horn shark uses its sense of smell to locate animals such as sea urchins and shellfish on which it feeds. They are caught with its sharp front teeth and crushed with flat teeth in the back of its mouth.

Downward-directed nostrils

This shark grows to about 3 ft (1 m)

NIGHT FEEDER
The lesser-spotted dogfish lives near land in water up to 328 ft (100 m) deep. During the day it hides among seaweed. At night it searches for shellfish and small fish.

TEETH

CUTTING EDGES
Variations in the teeth shapes of different species probably reflect differences in prey or hunting techniques. Sharks that feed on large fish or mammals usually have triangular teeth with serrated, sawlike edges.

GREAT WHITE SHARK

Serrated edge of tooth

MAKO SHARK

TIGER SHARK

LEMON SHARK

SWIFT HUNTERS
Blue sharks swim fast enough to prey on active fish such as mackerel. They are known as "blue whalers" because they sometimes gather in feeding frenzies around whale carcasses, their favorite food.

Snout turns up as shark attacks

BLUE SHARK WITH PREY

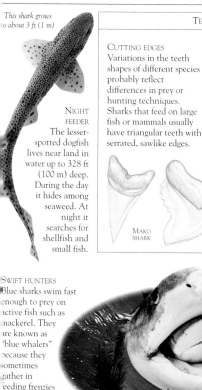

MATING AND FERTILIZATION

WHEN SOME MALE AND FEMALE sharks meet, the male chases and bites the female, encouraging her to mate. Sharks' mating behavior ensures that, unlike bony fish, the eggs are fertilized inside the female. In some species, the female lays eggs; in others, the young develop inside their mother – while some sharks are capable of both.

Males are usually smaller than their mates

MATING
Small male sharks, such as dogfish mate by winding their flexible body around the female. Some larger sharks mate side to side. Females often have thicker skin than the males' teeth to prevent injury during courtship.

REPRODUCTIVE ORGANS
Male sharks have a pair of claspers that are formed from part of the pelvic fins. During mating one of them is inserted into the female opening, called the cloaca. Sperm is released into the female to fertilize the eggs.

Cloaca

FEMALE PELVIC FINS

Clasper

MALE PELVIC FINS

EGG CASES

Shark eggs have a large egg yolk that is protected in a horny or leathery case. Female horn sharks lay spiral egg cases which they wedge into clefts in rocks for safety from other creatures.

SPIRAL EGG CASE OF HORN SHARK

Embryo dogfish inside an egg case

EMBRYO DEVELOPMENT

Sharks take up to a year to develop. When a pup hatches, it is at least 4 in (10 cm) long. As a result, it stands a better chance of survival than one of the many tiny young produced by most bony fish.

The embryo is nourished with a large yolk sac

HIDING PLACE

Most dogfish lay their eggs in dense beds of seaweed. The curly, ribbonlike ends on the corners of the egg cases tangle with seaweed fronds and are held safely. The movement of the water brings oxygen to the developing embryo.

DEVELOPMENT OF YOUNG

IN SOME SHARKS, the female produces thin-shelled eggs, which remain inside her body until they hatch. Sometimes baby sharks hatch at an early stage, but do not leave their mother's body. Each one continues to grow, feeding on its egg's large yolk sac.

LEMON SHARK

NEW PUP
When a lemon shark pup leaves its mother's body, it is still connected to her by its umbilical cord and the placenta, which has still to be expelled. The cord breaks when the pup swims away. Once free, it fends for itself and has no contact with its mother or other family members.

Newborn lemon shark pup

Umbilical cord attached to pup

Cream colored underside

DOGFISH PUPS
Dogfish pups grow fast for the first few years of their life. Later their growth slows, though they never stop growing completely. Some kinds of dogfish live for up to 25 years.

BIRTH FOR SURVIVAL

Birth is usually a rapid process to protect the newborn pup from enemies waiting to take advantage of a female or young in difficulty. Remoras are often nearby, waiting for the afterbirth, which they eat quickly. This reduces the likelihood of predators – including other sharks – being attracted to the birth scene.

TAIL FIRST
As a precaution against complications during birth, sharks are born tail first. The pup stands a better chance of survival if its head is still protected by its mother's body.

Pair of dogfish ups 10 days old and 4 in (10 cm) long

Soon the pups will feed on small creatures, such as shrimps

ENDANGERED NEWBORN
Game fishermen deliberately pursue female sharks since they are generally larger than males. Sometimes the trauma of being caught results in the female giving birth early to a litter of pups.

BONNETHEAD
SHARK PUPS

THE BODY CLOCK

ALL ANIMALS LIVE to rhythms dictated by the sun and the seasons. These are translated into patterns of behavior such as sleeping, breeding, and migrating. Even the lives of deep-sea sharks are regulated by their body clocks.

SLEEPER
SHARK

It used to be thought that sharks had to swim in order to breathe, but this is not true. The greenland shark and its close relatives are known as "sleeper sharks" because as well as being generally inactive, they spend a lot of time on the seabed, apparently asleep.

The greenland shark is a deep-water "sleeper"

SLEEPING FACTS

• Dreaming has been observed in bony fish, but not yet in sharks.

• The basking shark is probably the only plankton eater that hibernates. The others live where the food supply is less seasonal.

WINTER DOZE

In winter, when the supply of plankton falls, basking sharks hibernate. A number have been caught in trawl and when examined found to have lost their gill rakers New ones grow for the spring flush of plankton.

FAST ASLEEP

Nurse sharks are among several kinds of reef sharks known to rest for long periods on the seafloor. They appear to be breathing slowly, but if disturbed will swim off in a flurry as though awakened from a deep sleep.

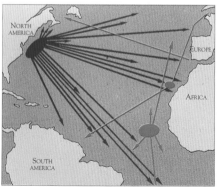

BLUE SHARK

Blue sharks do not sleep on the seabed

MIGRATION RHYTHM

Blue sharks migrate each year, moving between breeding and feeding grounds at definite times of the year. Like other oceanic sharks, blue sharks may rest without sinking to the bottom.

GREATEST TRAVELER

Tagging, mainly in the US, has shown that some blue sharks cover more than 3,726 miles (6,000 km) a year. More work remains to be done before the movements of different populations can be fully understood.

NORTH AMERICA

EUROPE

AFRICA

SOUTH AMERICA

RELEASE OF BLUE SHARKS

 TAGGING RELEASE
AREAS OFF US COAST

TAGGING RELEASE
AREAS ELSEWHERE

FRIENDS AND FOES

SHARKS HAVE FEW natural enemies, but many creatures known as commensals live close to, or are attached to, large sharks. Some of these creatures are able to live without the shark, unlike parasites such as tapeworms, that cannot survive away from their host's body.

Tentacle

Head

Suction pad

REMORAS

Remoras are sometimes called "shark suckers" because they attach themselves to a shark with a ridged sucker on top of their heads. They may feed on the shark's food scraps and are thought to aid the shark by also feeding on tiny parasites lodged in its skin.

TAPEWORMS

Inside the gut of a shark live hundreds of parasites called tapeworms. They feed on digested food and can grow up to 1 ft (30 cm) long.

PILOT FISH

In tropical waters, agile pilot fish swim below sharks. They do not, as their name suggests, guide the shark, but benefit from the protection gained by traveling with large sharks.

SHARK PARASITES

SKIN FEEDERS
Copepods are small relatives of crabs and form part of the plankton of the sea. Some become parasites on a shark's skin or gills, attaching themselves with adhesive pads and feeding on skin secretions.

FEMALE COPEPOD

MALE COPEPOD

EYE SPY
This crustacean is a parasite that feeds on the surface of the eyes of greenland sharks. It may damage its host's vision but may also attract small fish for the shark to eat.

Egg sac contains thousands of eggs

EYE SPY

SHARP CLAWS
This copepod hangs on to the shark's skin, feeding partly on blood. Basking sharks are thought to rid themselves of the irritation by leaping out of the sea.

Abdomen

Soft shell

HANGERS ON
Many large oceanic animals carry barnacles. The rootlets on the fleshy stalk of the barnacle feeds on body fluids.

BARNACLE

DOLPHIN VERSUS SHARK
It is thought that dolphins drive sharks away, but this is not necessarily true. However, the bottlenose dolphin has been trained by scientists in Florida to chase and attack sharks. During these experiments, the dolphin appeared able to distinguish one shark species from another.

When sharks and dolphins share an aquarium, they usually ignore each other

BOTTLENOSE DOLPHIN

SHARKS AND HUMANS

FEAR AND LOATHING

THE SHARK IS A POWERFUL symbol of terror, and sharks have traditionally been regarded as fearsome sea beasts to be hunted and killed without mercy. Sailors once believed that sharks preferred human flesh to all other and, even today, many regard all sharks as potential man-eaters.

HOLLYWOOD PARANOIA
The 1975 film *Jaws*, about a "killer" great white shark, scared audiences out of the water, and fueled worldwide hatred and fear of sharks. However, Peter Benchley, the author of the novel *Jaws*, now supports shark conservation.

ARTIST'S IMPRESSION
This engraving of a shark cast onto a beach in France was created more than 100 years ago. The mixture of features in the illustration – size of a great white, tail shape of a thresher – suggests that the artist was working from a description, not life.

FEEDING FRENZY

This shipwreck was the front cover of a Paris magazine in 1906. It illustrated one of sailors' most common fears – that of sharks in a feeding frenzy, swarming around a sinking ship, picking off survivors one by one.

Le Petit Parisien

SANTA MARIA

Columbus sailed this ship

BAD OMEN

Disease was common among early explorers, and dead bodies were often thrown overboard, which sometimes attracted sharks. Superstitious sailors believed that the presence of sharks foretold further deaths.

SHIPWRECK CASUALTIES CAUSED BY SHARKS

Tragedies at sea are a rare occurence, but are made much worse by sharks. During World War II, many lives were lost when sharks closed in on wounded and struggling sailors.

SHIP	DATE	PASSENGERS AND CREW	NUMBER LOST
Valerian	1926	104	84
Principessa Mafalda	1927	1,259	314
Cape San Juan	1943	1,429	981
Indianapolis	1945	1,199	883
Ganges Ferry Boat	1975	190	50+

SUPERSTITION FACTS

• Sailors falsely believed that sharks preferred the taste of people of their own nationality.

• Sailors used to take revenge on any shark they caught by torturing it to death.

SHARK ATTACK

NOBODY KNOWS why sharks sometimes attack people; most sharks are not dangerous and ignore humans unless threatened or provoked. Experts are unable to agree on the number of deaths caused by sharks.

Outer plastic casing

Casing of steel laths

Stainless steel ball bearings

Aluminum core

SHALLOW WATER
Attacks on humans often take place close to the shore in shallow water. This is probably because the majority of people are found swimming and paddling in this area.

BITE METER
By measuring the depth of the indentations when this device is placed inside a piece of bait, it is possible to determine the strength of a shark's bite.

SEAL FROM BELOW

SURFER

MISTAKEN IDENTITY
More men than women fall victim to shark attack. The reason for this is likely to be that men are more likely to swim alone in deep water. More men than women surf, and sharks can easily mistake a surfer for a seal, which is part of their natural diet.

PUBLIC ENEMY

The tiger shark is large and powerful enough to attack most sea creatures. Its diet includes seals, dolphins, sea snakes, hammerhead sharks, and turtles. Many humans have been killed by this shark.

RIVER MENACE

Bull sharks are dreaded in many parts of the tropics because they venture up rivers, posing a real threat to wildlife and humans alike.

GREAT HUNTER

The great white is deservedly the most feared shark of all. It can swim fast enough to jump right out of the water and is large enough to attack any animal in the sea. It has even been known to attack and sink small boats.

Fatalities

A person is more likely to be struck by lightning than attacked by a shark. Although experts disagree, it has been suggested that since 1940 there have been an average of only 28 attacks each year, one-third of which were fatal, worldwide. These figures include attacks made by sharks in self-defense or by those that were caught or harrassed in some way.

GREENLAND

NORTH AMERICA

ATLANTIC OCEAN

There are many recorded attacks in the West Indies

SOUTH AMERICA

ATTACK GEOGRAPHY
Almost all shark attacks take place in warm seas as few sharks live in cold water. On the map opposite, shark attacks are indicated in orange. Where the color is darker there is a higher incidence of attack in that area.

PACIFIC OCEAN

Few attacks recorded in this area

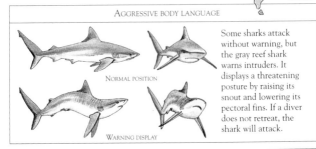

AGGRESSIVE BODY LANGUAGE

NORMAL POSITION

WARNING DISPLAY

Some sharks attack without warning, but the gray reef shark warns intruders. It displays a threatening posture by raising its snout and lowering its pectoral fins. If a diver does not retreat, the shark will attack.

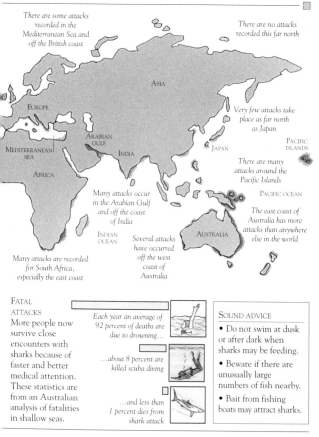

There are some attacks recorded in the Mediterranean Sea and off the British coast

There are no attacks recorded this far north

ASIA

EUROPE

Very few attacks take place as far north as Japan

PACIFIC ISLANDS

ARABIAN GULF

MEDITERRANEAN SEA

JAPAN

INDIA

AFRICA

There are many attacks around the Pacific Islands

PACIFIC OCEAN

Many attacks occur in the Arabian Gulf and off the coast of India

The east coast of Australia has more attacks than anywhere else in the world

INDIAN OCEAN

AUSTRALIA

Several attacks have occurred off the west coast of Australia

Many attacks are recorded for South Africa, especially the east coast

FATAL ATTACKS

More people now survive close encounters with sharks because of faster and better medical attention. These statistics are from an Australian analysis of fatalities in shallow seas.

Each year an average of 92 percent of deaths are due to drowning...

...about 8 percent are killed scuba diving

...and less than 1 percent dies from shark attack

SOUND ADVICE

• Do not swim at dusk or after dark when sharks may be feeding.

• Beware if there are unusually large numbers of fish nearby.

• Bait from fishing boats may attract sharks.

DEFENSE

ALL KINDS OF DEVICES – nets, repellents, electrical barriers, air bubbles – have been specially designed to protect swimmers and divers from the dangers of shark attack. Few, if any, have proved entirely successful, and some have proved dangerous to other sea creatures.

SHARK NET
Popular swimming beaches are often secured against sharks with mesh nets. Nets are costly and need constant maintenance, and unfortunately also trap many harmless creatures such as turtles, rays, and dolphins.

ARMOR SUIT
Some divers at risk from large, active sharks wear protective suits made of steel mesh, like medieval chain-mail armor. The suit prevents a shark's teeth from penetrating the diver's body, though there may be severe bruising from the shark's jaws.

DETAIL OF SHARK SUIT WITH TOOTH OF GREAT WHITE

CAGE PROTECTION

Some of the most dramatic pictures of sharks have been shot by underwater filmmakers enclosed by thick, metal cages. A shark's ability to detect underwater electric fields has possibly been the cause of numerous attacks on cages.

A bangstick can be effective in experienced hands

SHARK SCREEN BAG

The shark screen bag was developed to protect potential victims such as shipwrecked sailors or ditched airman from sharks. It disguises the shape of a person and keeps telltale scents from cruising sharks.

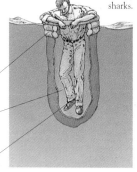

Three inflatable collars keep bag afloat

Scents and any blood kept in bag

No dangling legs to attract shark

SHARK WEAPON

A bangstick is a gun that fires bullets or a small explosive charge to defend divers from a shark attack. It is a more effective weapon than a spear gun, which does not always deter large sharks.

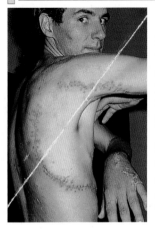

SURVIVORS

SHARK ATTACKS are not universally fatal. Most survivors have been physically fit and have remained calm during the attack. They have also been swimming near friends or within reach of a boat. Some people have survived by fighting back – attacking the shark's eyes with their bare hands.

MIRACULOUS RECOVERY

Australian diver Rodney Fox was taking part in a spearfishing competition near Adelaide in 1963 when he was attacked by a great white shark. His upper body was badly crushed and torn. He was rushed to the hospital, where he received 462 stitches in a 4-hour operation.

Surfers lying on their boards are an easy target

SURVIVAL FACTS

• Most sharks will only strike once.

• Blood loss and shock are the most dangerous effects of shark bites.

• About one-quarter of all attacks kill the victim.

LUCKY ESCAPE

Surfers can be at risk from sharks, athough few are attacked. This surfer's board was bitten by a 10–13 ft (3–4 m) shark near a coral reef in Hawaii.

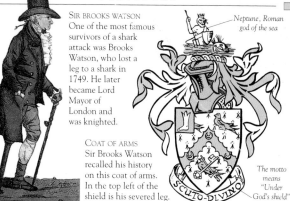

SIR BROOKS WATSON
One of the most famous survivors of a shark attack was Brooks Watson, who lost a leg to a shark in 1749. He later became Lord Mayor of London and was knighted.

Neptune, Roman god of the sea

COAT OF ARMS
Sir Brooks Watson recalled his history on this coat of arms. In the top left of the shield is his severed leg.

The motto means "Under God's shield"

CLOSE CALL
Valerie Taylor is a shark expert who has watched and filmed sharks for many years. In the photograph above she has been bitten on the leg. She was not seriously injured but still needed hospital treatment.

FORGIVING DIVER
Henri Bource lost a leg off the coast of Australia, where he was attacked by a great white in 1964. He still dives and does not blame the shark for its natural behavior.

FOLKLORE

THE INHABITANTS of some Pacific Islands regard certain sharks as gods, or spirits of their ancestors. Ancient Polynesians often believed that sharks were spirits sent by sorcerers to bring death and ill fortune. In some parts of West Africa, the shark is sacred and if one is accidentally killed, sacrificial rites must be performed.

SHARK/
BONITO
This charm, from Ulawa in the Solomon Islands, is of a bonito fish on one side and a shark on the other. Hunters carried carvings like these in their canoes, hoping to attract the bonito and repel large sharks.

The bonito hunting ritual was an annual event

Carving made of wood, inlaid with pearl

LATE-19TH-CENTURY
SHARK CHARM

Sharklike head

FOLKLORE FACTS

• Some Pacific Islanders believed that sharks would protect and save them from drowning.

• In Borneo, to stop babies from crying, the saw from a sawfish is covered in cloth and hung over the cradle.

SEA SPIRIT
Solomon Islanders believed that when people died their ghosts inhabited the bodies of sharks. This sea spirit has a head with fins like a shark. It was probably used to protect its maker from danger when fishing at sea.

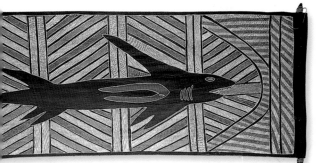

BARK PAINTING
This painting of a shark by the Yirrakala people of the Northern Territory, Australia, shows the huge two-lobed liver. Sharks were important to many native people as a source of food and oil.

Early-20th-century rattle from Papua New Guinea for attracting sharks

Rattle made from coconut shells

SHARK MASK
Native Americans from Alaska carve animal masks for use on ceremonial occasions. This mask is of a ground shark with a frog in its mouth. It is made of painted wood and leather, inlaid with abalone shell.

RATTLES
Some Pacific Islanders hunt sharks as a test of strength and manhood; others use the shark skin and teeth for decoration and weapons. The shark is lured using underwater rattles.

SHARK DIRECTORY

MACKEREL SHARKS

THE GREAT WHITE, the porbeagle, and the mako are collectively known as mackerel sharks. Powerful, fast swimmers, they feed on many kinds of prey. All of them are able to push their jaws forward, to tear chunks from prey too large to be swallowed whole. Little is known about their breeding behavior or migratory habits.

GREAT WHITE

WARM-BLOODED
Porbeagle sharks prefer more temperate seas and may be seen near the British and North American coasts in summer. They are heavily built and partly warm-blooded, being able to keep their body temperature several degrees higher than their surroundings.

MACKEREL FACTS

• Mackerel sharks make spectacular leaps when hooked by game fishermen.

• Unborn makos and porbeagles survive in the uterus by eating the unfertilized eggs.

• Normally only two pups are born at a time.

Single-keeled tail of the mako

Double-keeled tail of the porbeagle

TAIL FINS
The tail lobes of mackerel sharks are nearly equal in size. Mako and porbeagles have small stabilizing keels at the base of their tail. The keel probably helps the fish to stay on course when making tight turns.

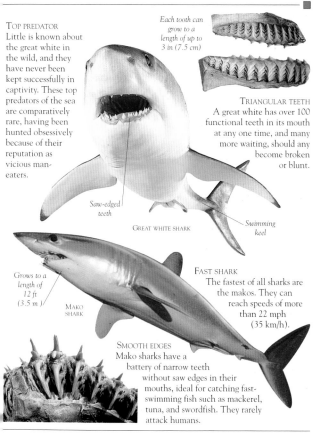

TOP PREDATOR
Little is known about the great white in the wild, and they have never been kept successfully in captivity. These top predators of the sea are comparatively rare, having been hunted obsessively because of their reputation as vicious man-eaters.

Each tooth can grow to a length of up to 3 in (7.5 cm)

TRIANGULAR TEETH
A great white has over 100 functional teeth in its mouth at any one time, and many more waiting, should any become broken or blunt.

Saw-edged teeth

GREAT WHITE SHARK

Swimming keel

Grows to a length of 12 ft (3.5 m)

MAKO SHARK

FAST SHARK
The fastest of all sharks are the makos. They can reach speeds of more than 22 mph (35 km/h).

SMOOTH EDGES
Mako sharks have a battery of narrow teeth without saw edges in their mouths, ideal for catching fast-swimming fish such as mackerel, tuna, and swordfish. They rarely attack humans.

HAMMERS AND THRESHERS

THE HAMMERHEAD and the thresher shark are not closely related, but both are easy to recognize: one for its extraordinary head; the other for its long tail, which may make up half its length. The teeth of close relatives of hammerheads and thresher sharks have been found in rocks at least 60 million years old.

LONG TAIL
Most threshers are surface swimmers, hunting small fish such as herring or sardines. Thresher pups may be 5 ft (1.5 m) long at birth. One species has very large eyes and lives in deep water.

Upper lobe of tail may be half the size of body

Can grow up to 20 ft (6 m) long

Threshers weigh about 1,000 lb (450 kg)

THRESHER SHARK

BONNET HEAD
The shovel-shaped head, with eyes and nostrils on the outer edge, marks the bonnet shark as a small relative of the great hammerheads. It often comes into shallow bays to hunt small fish, crabs, and shrimps. Like all hammerheads, it produces live young.

BONNET SHARK

Gill slits

Mouth is located under the head

SENSORY HEAD
Hammerheads swing their heads from side to side as they swim, testing the water for the presence of stingrays, their main prey. Sometimes the sting of a ray will become embedded in a shark's jaws, causing its teeth to grow abnormally.

HAMMERHEAD SHARK

Large number of ampullae of Lorenzini

Eye positioned on side of head

HAMMER SCHOOLS
Hammerheads hunt as individuals at night, and by day swim together in large numbers. In such a school, there are about four females to every male, but nobody has ever observed hammerheads mating.

LETHAL TAIL
Thresher sharks are thought to work in pairs, lashing their tails to frighten groups of fish into a tight pack that can be caught easily. Threshers are sought after by game fishermen, as they are exciting prey. However, they can inflict severe injuries with their powerful tails.

REQUIEM SHARKS

SAILORS IN DAYS GONE BY did not name this group of sharks because of any connection with death. They called them requiem, or "rest," sharks because they were often seen in fair weather. Some requiems live in the open ocean, while others, such as those shown here, are found close to the shore.

WARNING SIGNAL

Divers may encounter gray reef sharks since they are often found in lagoons and on the outer edges of reefs. They are not usually dangerous, but may be territorial. If it feels threatened, a gray reef shark will warn intruders by arching its back into an aggressive posture.

Long upper lobe of silky shark

Measures 8 ft (2.5 m) in length

Grows to over 10 ft (3 m) in length

LAGOON DWELLER
The lemon shark is often found in shallow lagoons. It eats crabs, octopuses, and seabirds. It also eats stingrays, and often has stings embedded in its mouth as a result. It is born in shallow water where it stays for some years before gradually venturing out into open seas.

LEMON SHARK

SILKY SHARK

SILKY SMOOTH
Named because of its small and smooth dermal denticles, the silky shark's sides do not have the rough feel of those of most other sharks. It is one of the most common species of shark, often taking tuna from the nets of fishermen.

Dorsal fin sticks out of the water in shallows

Body length can reach 6 ft (1.8 m)

Denticles of silky shark are only 0.01 in (0.25 mm) across

AGGRESSIVE SPECIES
Often lying in reef pools only 2 ft (60 cm) deep, blacktip reef sharks are not to be trifled with. They can become aggressive if they detect fishing bait, and may attack people.

REQUIEM FACTS

• Females store their mate's sperm until the next year, when the eggs are fertilized.

• Requiems produce about 14 young in a litter.

• Requiem pups grow faster than other sharks.

More requiems

All requiem sharks shown here are large species that may be dangerous. The blue shark lives in almost all the oceans of the world and is responsible for some attacks on shipwrecked sailors. Tiger sharks are found only in warm seas, close to the shore. Bull sharks sometimes venture into freshwater.

BLUE SHARK

TRAVELING HUNTER
Blue sharks are the great travelers of the shark world, covering huge distances each year. They do not dive deeply for food, but hunt almost any kind of surface-living fish. They particularly like whale meat and are known to gather in "feeding frenzies" when they find a whale carcass.

REQUIEM FACTS

• The distinctive stripes on a tiger shark fade as the shark ages.

• Female blue sharks have skin thicker than the length of the male's teeth to prevent injury during courtship.

OCEANIC WHITETIP SHARK

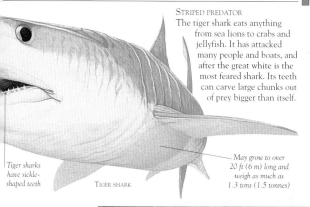

STRIPED PREDATOR
The tiger shark eats anything
from sea lions to crabs and
jellyfish. It has attacked
many people and boats, and
after the great white is the
most feared shark. Its teeth
can carve large chunks out
of prey bigger than itself.

*Tiger sharks
have sickle-
shaped teeth*

TIGER SHARK

*May grow to over
20 ft (6 m) long and
weigh as much as
1.3 tons (1.5 tonnes)*

ADAPTABILITY
Bull sharks have
developed an ability to
maintain a balance
between the salt
content of their bodies
and the freshwater of
a river or lake system.
Some bull sharks may
spend a large portion of
their lives in freshwater.

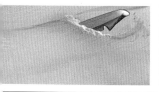

WHITE-TIPPED SHARK
The oceanic whitetip shark is a slow-
moving, abundant species that grows to a
length of 13 ft (4 m). It is a fearless and
very dangerous species found in most
parts of the world. This shark is despised
by tuna fishermen and whalers beacuse of
the harm it inflicts on their catches.

CARPET AND NURSE SHARKS

MOST KINDS OF CARPET and nurse sharks live in Australia and east Asian waters. They live on the seabed, and all are sluggish swimmers. Most are small, with sharp teeth for eating small fish and invertebrates. Nurse sharks were named by early explorers after an ancient word meaning "big fish."

Long, narrow tail

Brownbanded sharks are found in Arabia, Japan, and Australia

CARPET SHARKS
The brownbanded shark is a type of a carpet shark. It sometimes ventures into harbors and is common on reefs. It can survive out of water for up to 12 hours if stranded by low tide.

Epaulets live on the Great Barrier Reef, Australia

TASSEL DISGUISE
Wobbegongs lie half buried in the sand, camouflaged by their speckled colors. Their front teeth are sharp and daggerlike. If food is scarce, these sharks are able to clamber out of the water and cross a reef, from one rock pool to another.

Skin is camouflaged to blend with the seabed

WOBBEGONG

BROWNBANDED SHARK

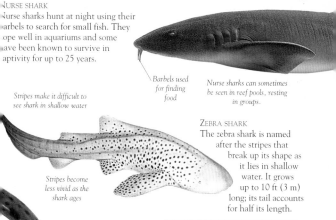

NURSE SHARK
Nurse sharks hunt at night using their barbels to search for small fish. They cope well in aquariums and some have been known to survive in captivity for up to 25 years.

Barbels used for finding food

Nurse sharks can sometimes be seen in reef pools, resting in groups.

Stripes make it difficult to see shark in shallow water

ZEBRA SHARK
The zebra shark is named after the stripes that break up its shape as it lies in shallow water. It grows up to 10 ft (3 m) long; its tail accounts for half its length.

Stripes become less vivid as the shark ages

EPAULET SHARK
This shark is common and harmless to humans. It searches for food in shallow pools. Like the wobbegong it can "walk" from pool to pool, using its pectoral fins to haul itself along.

EPAULET SHARK

NOT A REAL NURSE
Although the sandtiger shark is known as the gray nurse shark in Australia, it is far more active than the nurse sharks. Usually not aggressive unless provoked, its distinctive, ragged teeth can cause serious injury.

CATSHARKS

ONE-THIRD of all sharks belong to the catshark family. Small, slender fish, with two dorsal fins set well back on the body, most are found in deep water, where they live on the seabed. A few kinds are known from only one specimen, and it is likely that more will be discovered in the future.

First dorsal fin is placed well back on the body

Does not have a nictitating eyelid (see page 116)

Only about 20 in (50 cm) in length

LONGNOSE CATSHARK

Very long tail fin

DEEP-SEA SHARK
The longnose catshark lives off the west coast of North America. It is a deep-water species that has been recorded as deep as 6,250 ft (1,900 m), but is rarely found above 3,000 ft (900 m). Many deep-sea catsharks are brownish in color and so are well camouflaged for their murky environment.

Grows to about 3 ft (90 cm) long

Blotchy skin and black-banded neck

VARIED CATSHARK
This bottom-living catshark prefers a sandy seabed and is related to the carpet sharks. It is not often seen, though it is occasionally caught in lobster traps.

VARIED CATSHARK

Lives at depths of 526 ft (160 m)

TEETH

Swell sharks have wide mouths lined with a large number of tiny, sharp teeth. Their main food is small fish and bait used for catching lobster.

SWELL SHARK TEETH

GULF CATSHARK

In some species, females keep their egg cases inside their bodies until the young are nearly ready to hatch. This shark lives in the sea south of Australia.

Dense color with white spots

CATSHARK FACTS

• Some species are similar to fossils over 100 million years old.

• Catsharks have very flabby bodies.

• Pups have two rows of large dermal denticles to help them out of their egg case.

SWELL PROTECTION

The swell shark is nocturnal. It rests in crevices or among giant kelp during the day. If disturbed, it swallows water or air, and swells out its body to about twice its normal size. This makes it almost impossible to pull from its hiding place.

Groups sometimes rest lying on top of one another

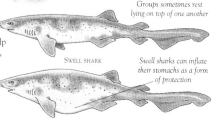

SWELL SHARK

Swell sharks can inflate their stomachs as a form of protection

DOGFISH

MANY KINDS OF SMALL sharks are known as dogfish. Some, like the spiny dogfish, are related to deep-water sharks. They live near the seabed, often close to land, but have been known to venture into freshwater, traveling a short distance up rivers. Dogfish are an important source of food and are fished all over the globe.

Grows to about 7 ft (2 m) in length

Some species emit an unpleasant smell

Feeds on bottom-living invertebrates

Sharp nose

TOPE

Can live for over 40 years

TOPE
During summer, tope live in small groups and the females may give birth to as many as 50 pups. Tope are not fished commercially, but some anglers specialize in catching them – there are even tope clubs.

COMMON SPECIES
The lesser-spotted dogfish is one of the most common sharks in western European seas. It is found on sandbanks where there are plenty of sheltering seaweeds. The females lay their egg capsules among the weeds to keep them safe.

STARRY SMOOTHHOUND

STARRY SMOOTH

Starry smoothhounds are sluggish sharks that live in shallow seas in many parts of the world. They are so named because of the small, white spots that break the dark shade of their sides and back. One species that lives off the US coast is able to change its color from gray to pearly white, taking about two days to complete the transition.

Females give birth to up to 40 pups at a time

Large pectoral fins

Most of its time is spent cruising on the seabed, searching for food

SPOTTED SKIN

The leopard shark gets its name from its golden, blotched skin. Like some other carpet sharks, it has a flexible body that allows it to turn around in small spaces. It feeds mainly on clams, using its flat-topped teeth.

Grows to about 5 ft (1.5 m)

LEOPARD SHARK

DOGFISH FACTS

• Dogfish were named by fishermen who thought their teeth resembled those of dogs.

• Dogfish are sold for food in Europe as rock salmon or huss, and in Australia as flake.

It is a very hardy species and thrives in aquariums

Grows to about 3 ft (1 m) in length

LESSER-SPOTTED DOGFISH

PLANKTON EATERS

THE THREE LARGEST FISH in the sea – the whale shark, basking shark, and megamouth shark – are all harmless, docile creatures that feed mainly on plankton. All have more than a thousand gill rakers that strain the current for food and an immense liver that contains a substantial amount of oil.

SEA SOUP
Plankton is made up of floating plants and animals that are unable to swim against the ocean currents. A few of these animals, such as jellyfish may be big, but most are tiny. Some, such as the larvae of crabs and sea urchins, are only part of the plankton "soup" for a short time before growing into adult animals.

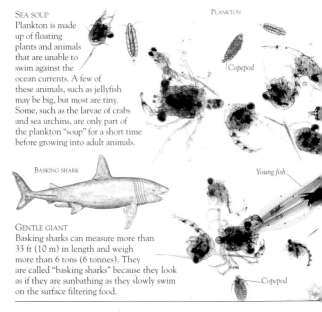

PLANKTON

Copepod

Young fish

Copepod

BASKING SHARK

GENTLE GIANT
Basking sharks can measure more than 33 ft (10 m) in length and weigh more than 6 tons (6 tonnes). They are called "basking sharks" because they look as if they are sunbathing as they slowly swim on the surface filtering food.

INSIDE THE MOUTH

Basking sharks use the same action to feed and to breathe. Bars of cartilage in the throat support the gills and gill rakers. Water flows into the mouth, where it is strained through the gill rakers to filter out food particles. It is then pushed over the gills, where oxygen and carbon dioxide are exchanged.

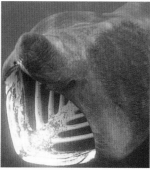

BASKING SHARK

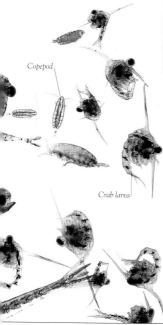

Copepod

Crab larva

FOOD SIEVE

Each comblike gill raker is made of keratin, a material similar to human fingernails. Basking sharks shed their gill rakers in winter when the plankton supply diminishes, but grow new ones in the spring.

GILL RAKERS OF A BASKING SHARK

Whale and megamouth shark

Whale and megamouth sharks are plankton
eaters that live in tropical waters. Both are
enormous: the whale shark is the largest of
all fish and may grow to a length of 59 ft
(18 m) and weigh up to 44 tons (40 tonnes).
The megamouth measures more than 13 ft (4 m).
Anatomically, the megamouth is more closely
related to the great white
than to other
filter feeders.

OPEN WIDE
The whale shark's mouth is small
compared with that of a basking
shark. The gill arches are connected
by gristly bars that support mesh filters
that trap plankton.

*Open mouth of the
whale shark*

TINY TEETH
Whale sharks have a large
number of tiny teeth that serve
no function since they cannot
chew or tear food. However,
divers can be bruised if an arm or
a leg becomes caught on the
shark's teeth.

WHALE SHARK TEETH

ANCESTRAL BEHAVIOR
Whale sharks have been observed more or less
vertical in the water when feeding on small
fish such as anchovies. This unusual feeding
posture probably harks back to the
habits of their ancient ancestors.

DIVER FRIENDLY

Whale sharks are placid animals that will tolerate divers holding on to their fins. They lay the world's largest eggs, which are at least 40 times as big as a chicken's egg. The embryos of whale sharks may grow to more than 14 in (35 cm) long.

Longer upper lobe of tail

Silvery luminescence around the mouth is thought to attract shrimps and other food

NEW SPECIES

The megamouth shark escaped the attention of science until 1976 when one was accidentally caught off the coast of Hawaii by a US research vessel. It was hauled aboard so scientists could examine the specimen in detail.

MEGAMOUTH SHARK

DEEP-SEA DWELLERS

THE AVERAGE DEPTH of the oceans is about 11,500 ft (3,500 m). Most of this vast bulk of water is cold, and largely unknown. There is no light in the oceans below 3,300 ft (1,000 m), and at these depths, fish tend to be small because food is scarce. Many species use light signals to communicate with one another, to lure prey, or to find a mate.

BLACKBELLY LANTERN SHARK

BLACKBELLY LANTERN SHARK
Lantern sharks have been found at depths of 6,500 ft (2,000 m). Like most deep-water fish, they have large eyes to make use of what little light there may be. They emit a bright green glow from light-producing organs along their flanks.

Second spine on dorsal fin

Large dorsal fin with spine

Black fin stripes

HUMANTIN
The humantin is sometimes called the prickly dogfish after its large and rough dermal denticles. Because it lives in deep water, it is rarely caught, but is easy to recognize by its unusual shape. It feeds on hard-shelled invertebrates.

HUMANTIN

Food is picked up with its thick, spongy lips

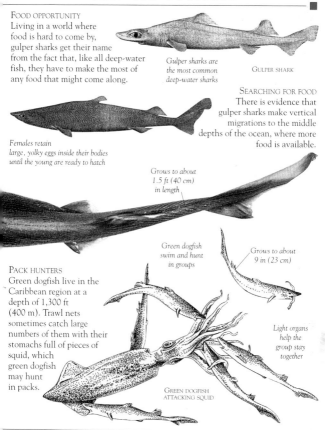

FOOD OPPORTUNITY
Living in a world where
food is hard to come by,
gulper sharks get their name
from the fact that, like all deep-water
fish, they have to make the most of
any food that might come along.

*Gulper sharks are
the most common
deep-water sharks*

GULPER SHARK

SEARCHING FOR FOOD
There is evidence that
gulper sharks make vertical
migrations to the middle
depths of the ocean, where more
food is available.

*Females retain
large, yolky eggs inside their bodies
until the young are ready to hatch*

*Grows to about
1.5 ft (40 cm)
in length*

*Green dogfish
swim and hunt
in groups*

*Grows to about
9 in (23 cm)*

PACK HUNTERS
Green dogfish live in the
Caribbean region at a
depth of 1,300 ft
(400 m). Trawl nets
sometimes catch large
numbers of them with their
stomachs full of pieces of
squid, which
green dogfish
may hunt
in packs.

*Light organs
help the
group stay
together*

GREEN DOGFISH
ATTACKING SQUID

STRANGE SHARKS

SOME OF THE MOST UNUSUAL sharks live in rarely
explored habitats. Some species are known by only
one or two specimens, so their behavior can only
be guessed at. Sometimes there may be clues, such
as the curious wounds in the bodies of seals and
whales – which turned out to be
the work of the
cookiecutter shark.

ODD BITE
Cookiecutters are only 20 in
(50 cm) long, yet they have
the largest teeth, compared
with their size, of any living
shark. They feed by gouging
round plugs of flesh from their victims.

*Disk-shaped bite
from cookiecutter*

*Flexible lips clamp
onto prey*

COOKIECUTTER

*This dwarf shark is only
about 6 in (15 cm) long*

*It is protected by a
spine on its first
dorsal fin*

DWARF SHARK
The dwarf shark is known
from very few specimens.
It lives in deep
water, in the
Pacific Ocean. It
seems likely that it
makes vertical
migrations, as it has
also been caught in shallow
seas. Like many deep-sea fish, it
has light organs on its underside.

SLEEPY SHARKS

Greenland sharks are sometimes called "sleepers" because they are sluggish sharks. They live in cold, northern waters – under the ice during the winter. They eat carrion, and large numbers may gather to gorge on a whale carcass. One is said to have been found with a reindeer in its stomach.

Greenland sharks are larger than most of their relatives

BIZARRE SHARK

The goblin shark was first discovered off the coast of Japan over 100 years ago, yet little is known about it. Goblin sharks live in water between 330–2,300 ft (100–700 m) deep.

GREENLAND SHARK

Undeveloped tail fin

Sensory pores on long snout detect prey

UNDERSIDE OF HEAD

The goblin, or "elfin," shark grows to about 13 ft (4 m) in length

Its flabby body suggests an inactive lifestyle

TOP SIDE OF HEAD

COOKIECUTTER FACTS

• Cookiecutters were named after the cookie-shaped bite they leave on their victims.

• Cookiecutters are one of the few animals that attack prey much larger than themselves.

SHARK ODDITIES

SHARKS ARE SUPREME evolutionary
opportunists, filling all kinds of roles and
thriving in almost all marine habitats.
Some even mimic the appearance
– and success – of other fish,
such as rays and sawfish, but
beneath their sometimes
strange surface appearance,
the true structure of the
shark remains.

*Equal-sized
teeth*

SAWFISH
TEETH

STARRY RAY
Rays have cartilaginous
skeletons and dermal denticles like sharks,
but have followed a separate evolutionary
path since the time of the dinosaurs.
The starry ray lives on the seabed in
cold waters around the coasts
of Europe and eastern
North America.

*Sawshark
teeth are
different sizes*

SAWFISH
Sawfish are
related to rays
but have long,
flattened snouts like
sawsharks. Sawfish teeth
are all the same size,
unlike those of sawsharks,
which differ in length.
Sawfish grow to more
than 33 ft (10 m)
in length.

SAWSHARK
Sawsharks stir up the
seabed with their long,
toothed snout, feeling
for small fish and crabs with their
barbels. Baby sawsharks' teeth are
covered with skin up to the time they
are born, so they don't injure their
mother or one another.

WELL HIDDEN
An angel shark is hard to see as it lies on the seabed. Its body is so flat that it appears no more than a low mound in the sand. Unlike a ray, it uses its tail rather than its large fins to swim.

ANGEL SHARK

Mouth at front of head

ANGEL SHARK
There are 13 different kinds of angel shark and all live in shallow, warm seas, though some migrate to warmer waters during the summer. They hunt at night in their own territories. Unlike rays, they have sharp teeth for feeding on shelled prey and small fish.

Large pectoral fin

Sandy-colored skin is well camouflaged for life on the seabed

UNDER THE SAND
Angel sharks disguise themselves by covering their bodies in sand.

Angel shark covers itself in sand

ODDITIES FACTS

• Angel shark is often sold as a substitute for shrimp or lobster.

• Like a ray, an angel shark has eyes on the top of its head so it can see while lying flat.

• The body length of Sawfish is ten times longer than sawsharks.

EVOLUTIONARY LEFTOVERS

TODAY'S SEAS provide an environment similar to that of the ancient oceans in which sharks evolved. Some sharks have become extinct, their places taken by more efficient species, but others have survived unchanged for millions of years. Several species were known only to science from fossils before the living animals were found.

SEVEN-GILLED SHARK
Some rare sharks have six or even seven gill openings. The way the jaws are attached to the skull, and the fact that there is little calcium hardening their vertebrae makes them similar to primitive sharks.

SEVEN-GILLED SHARK

Grows to almost 7 ft (2 m) in length

Eel-like body shape

LIVING FOSSIL
More than any other shark, the frilled shark can be called a living fossil. It has six gill slits, the first of which is very long and looks like a frilly collar. It is almost eel-like in shape, and certain features of its vertebrae, its blood system, and its lateral line are no longer found in modern sharks.

FRILLED SHARK

Short "bull face" of horn shark

HORN HABITS

The horn shark rests during the day, often in groups of several individuals. It hunts at night, using its sense of smell to find food. Though not closely related to the extinct *Hybodus*, it has large spines on the leading edge of its dorsal fins.

HORN SHARK

HORN FOSSIL

The earliest fossil of a horn shark dates back about 150 million years. Today, similar sharks feed on shelled prey, which they crush with flat-topped teeth much like those of ancient fossils.

DEEP-SEA HUNTER

The frilled shark is armed with about 300 teeth, set in 27 rows. Each tooth carries three sharp hooks, so prey stand little chance of escape.

FRILLED SHARK TEETH

EVOLUTIONARY FACTS

• Frilled sharks are found in deep water throughout the world, but are not common anywhere.

• Horn sharks use fin spines to burrow under rocks, searching for prey, which are often worn down to half their length.

SHARKS FOR THE FUTURE

DIVERSITY IN THE SEA

SINCE ANCIENT TIMES, sharks have been part of almost every marine environment, but today many species are threatened. Many people ask why the oceans need dangerous creatures such as sharks, but being major predators, sharks play an important role in preserving the balance of nature in the sea.

GULF CATSHARK

ABUNDANT SPECIES
There are more kinds of catshark than any other group of sharks, yet most of them are unfamiliar. They are usually small, few measuring more than 3 ft (1 m) in length, and often live on the seabed.

INDISCRIMINATE EATERS
The bull shark, alone among present-day sharks, regularly enters the freshwater of estuaries and rivers. It thus comes into regular contact with humans and can be dangerous. It will eat almost any flesh, fresh or carrion, and is also attracted to waste thrown into rivers.

TOP PREDATOR

Because humans fall within the size range of its usual food, the great white may attack bathers and surfers. As a result, it is more feared and hated than more common – and possibly more dangerous – sharks.

The great white is an endangered species

GREAT WHITE SHARK

BIG FISH

The largest of all fish, the whale shark sifts plankton from the sea with its gill rakers. It also eats small fish, which enables its worn gill rakers to regrow. It is possible that another plankton-feeder, the basking shark, hibernates to renew its gill rakers.

The whale shark has a smaller mouth than other plankton eaters

WHALE SHARK

SMALLEST SHARK

The lantern shark is the smallest of all sharks. It has been recorded at depths of 6,600 ft (2,000 m). Finding food and a mate is difficult at these cold, dark depths, but its light organs may help with both vital activities. It is possible that it hunts in groups.

SOUTHERN LANTERN SHARK

ENDANGERED SHARKS

SOME SPECIES of shark are rare because of exploitation by humans. All sharks breed slowly, some producing no more than two young a year, and many mature slowly, so that a depleted population cannot recover quickly.

LEFT TO DIE

Many sharks are seriously injured by game fishermen who hunt them for sport and leave them to die on the seafloor. Sometimes the fins are cut off a live shark to be sold. The body is then thrown back into the sea to die. In some parts of the West Indies and the Australian coast, the seabed is littered with corpses.

ENDANGERED YOUNG

Female sharks are larger than males, which makes them sought after by trophy hunters. Some species, such as blue sharks, swim into inshore waters to give birth. For every female caught, a litter of young has been lost – something that no animal species can withstand for long.

SHARK-TOOTH
NECKLACE FROM
NEW ZEALAND

*Necklaces made from
great white teeth can
fetch high prices*

TOURIST MEMENTOS
Some souvenirs seriously
threaten indigenous
wildlife. It is more than
likely that a shark
was slaughtered
to make this
necklace of
teeth.

ENDANGERED FACTS
• Humans kill up to
100 million sharks
every year.

• As slow breeders,
sharks cannot replace
such losses.

• Many species of
shark are already
endangered.

*Because of overfishing,
sharks are now rare
where they were once
abundant*

UNDER ATTACK
The piked dogfish
is one of many
small sharks caught
each year for food.
Recently in the North
Atlantic, the larger oceanic
sharks have come under similar
attack and have drastically
declined in numbers.

PRICELESS JAWS
Despite their high price, shark jaws are
popular with tourists, who severely
endanger the shark population by
buying them. However, attitudes may
be changing: for example, a recent
study in the Maldives estimated that a
living gray reef shark could generate
$2,500 in tourism. The same shark
dead would fetch only $24.

INDUSTRY

THE KILLING OF SHARKS for industrial use has a long history, since almost half the known species of shark have some commercial value. In the past, sharks' teeth were used as weapons, their skin was used as sandpaper, and their livers for oil. Today they are still hunted, but numbers are now in serious decline.

HAMMERHEAD TRAPPED IN NET

FISHING NETS
Sharks can easily become trapped in fishing nets used by trawlers or safety nets used to protect bathing beaches. Once entangled, it is almost impossible for them to escape. They often end up drowning because they cannot keep water flowing over their gills.

ENVIRONMENTAL POLLUTION
Some sharks have been found with plastic packaging straps caught around their bodies. As the shark grows, the plastic gradually cuts into its flesh, resulting in horrible injuries to its body.

Because sharks cannot swim backward, they are unable to free themselves from packing straps that become caught around their bodies

LIVER PILLS

Health pills made from shark's liver claim to reduce the incidence of heart disease and cancer, and to increase longevity. For many years, shark livers were used as a source of vitamins A and E until a synthetic alternative was discovered in the 1950's.

Shark-fin fibers look like noodles

SHARK-FIN SOUP

ASIAN DELICACY

Shark-fin soup is made from the cartilaginous fibers in the fin of a shark. After the fins are cut from the shark and hung to dry, they are soaked and repeatedly boiled to extract the fibers. Other ingredients are added to the soup to give it flavor.

Plastic that has cut into the shark's body

Tiger, dusky, and bull sharks have been found off the coast of Florida badly injured by plastic straps

COSMETICS

The gallbladder and part of the shark's liver have been shown to improve acne and other skin complaints. However, natural plant oils are just as effective for improving these skin conditions.

INDUSTRY FACTS

• As it becomes more affordable, shark-fin soup is increasing in popularity throughout the world.

• Drift nets used to catch squid in the North Pacific also catch about 1.8 million blue sharks each year.

TOURISM

ECOTOURISM, one of the fastest-growing tourism markets, could well be the key to some sharks' long-term survival. Sharks, swimming free in their own habitat, offer enormous economic potential as a tourist attraction.

SHARK PHOTOGRAPHY
Professional shark photographers often work from the protection of an underwater cage, particularly when filming a dangerous shark such as the great white. As a service for tourists, underwater safaris could give amateurs similar shelter and excitement.

Tail fluke of sperm whale off the coast of New Zealand

WHALE APPEAL
Whale watching is a valuable part of ecotourism. In some countries, it is now a bigger industry than hunting ever was. It is possible that shark-watching trips may also become a tourist attraction. Sharks are easily attracted using bait and unlike whales are less likely to be upset or distressed by the presence of humans.

IN THE RING
There are places where shark wrestling is staged as an attraction for tourists. While it apparently does little damage to the shark, it is one of the least desirable activities concerning tourism and sharks.

SHARK DIVES
Swimming with sharks is an exciting experience for the adventurous. Specialized tour operators can organize dives with hammerhead, reef, whale, and blue sharks – even the great white (which must be viewed from the safety of a strong cage).

MARINE AQUARIUM
Most aquariums show only small sharks, as big oceanic sharks are difficult to keep in captivity. The only great white ever kept in an aquarium had to be released after it repeatedly banged into the walls of its pool and became disoriented.

SHARKS IN SCIENCE

IN LABORATORIES in many parts of the world, teams of scientists are grappling with the intricacies of shark life, anatomy, and biochemistry. Much research centers on the fact that sharks appear to be unusually disease-free. The shark's physiological secrets may prove of great benefit to humankind.

DENTICLE RESEARCH

In the past, a shark's dermal denticles have provided information about teeth and their formation. More recently, scientists have come to believe that a shark's denticles move to affect water flow over its body. This may have potential applications in the field of ship and aircraft design.

DENTICLES
x 110 MAGNIFICATION

Ridges on the denticles help reduce drag

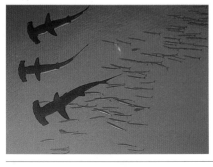

MONEY-SAVER

Tiny grooves on the dermal denticles of sharks such as hammerheads can reduce drag by up to 10 percent. Scientists are studying how these grooves work as a reduction in drag of only 1 or 2 percent could save the airline industry billions of dollars in fuel costs, as well as helping engineers design safer planes.

ANTIBIOTIC BREAKTHROUGH

Shark liver is a rich source of a steroid called squalamine. Its chief value seems to be as an antibiotic that may protect patients against bacteria, fungi, and other disease-causing organisms. It could also be useful in attacking bacteria that have become resistant to other drugs.

ARTIFICIAL SKIN

Here, in a medical laboratory, artificial skin grown from shark-fin cartilage is being used as a graft to heal a serious burn. Squalamine will increase its chance of success.

CURE FOR DISEASE

Besides being caught for food in large numbers, the spiny dogfish has contributed to our understanding of salt removal from the bloodstream. The mechanism that it employs to do this is proving useful as a way of treating the disease cystic fibrosis.

SPINY DOGFISH

SCIENCE FACTS

• Shark gall bladders have been used in the treatment of acne.

• Liver oil is still used in some cosmetics.

• Corneas from the eyes of sharks are used in some human transplant operations.

RESEARCH

ALTHOUGH HUMANS have had contact with sharks since prehistoric times, most research into their behavior is comparatively recent. Work with living sharks is concerned mainly with lifespan and migrations; it usually involves tagging or radio-tracking individuals for a short time.

TAGGING SHARKS

Baited hooks are used to catch a shark

The shark is carefully brought on board

REELING IN
A shark must be caught before it can be tagged. Most tagging is done by game fishermen who record the weight and size of the shark on special cards issued by research institutions.

TAGGING
The tag, which is a noncorrosive numbered disk or dart, is placed securely in the muscles just below the first dorsal fin. Should the shark be caught again in another part of the world, there is an address on the reverse side of the tag where it can be returned.

326

RELEASE
Once tagged, the shark is returned to the sea. If it is caught again, the catcher should inform the tagging authority so that information about the shark can be recorded and exchanged.

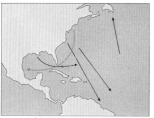

ATLANTIC SHARK MOVEMENTS

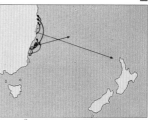

SHARK MOVEMENTS OFF AUSTRALIA

OCEAN MOVEMENTS

Few sharks are recovered, but some are known to have lived for as long as 20 years after they were tagged. These maps show shark movements tracked as a result of tagging on the east coasts of the US and Australia. Apart from the Port Jackson shark, the species tagged are fairly large and active. Small and deep-water sharks do not feature in these studies since they are hard to catch and follow.

SHARK KEY

WHALER

HAMMERHEAD

SANDBAR

TIGER

PORT JACKSON

MAKO

Fibers strengthen
the vertebra

Groups of rings
form bands that
show the
shark's age

Band

BASKING
SHARK
VERTEBRA

AGE RINGS

Sharks continue to grow throughout their lives, usually with seasonal spurts of growth. Scientists can assess the age and growth rates of sharks by treating the bones (vertebrae) of their backs with special chemicals.

PROTECTION

THE LARGE-SCALE destruction of sharks, mainly in the second half of this century, has led ecologists to pressure governments to protect both it and its environment. Despite opposition in some quarters, the killing of sharks is now controlled in many parts of the world.

GLOBAL EFFORTS
This map shows where the great white shark is now protected. Countries that are signatories to international conventions can halt trade in endangered species, thereby preventing slaughter in the name of tourism.

GREAT WHITE SHARK PROTECTED AREAS

FISHING BAN
The great white is a protected species off the east coast of Australia, California, South Africa, and the Maldives. Huge fines or jail are the penalty for breaking the ban.

GREAT WHITE SHARK

EXTINCT SPECIES

Hybodus was a common shark alive during the time of the dinosaurs, yet about 65 million years ago, it became extinct. However, *Hybodus* disappeared gradually as modern sharks evolved. Today, wanton killing of sharks by humans leaves no time for replacement.

Hybodus had a large spine in front of both its dorsal fins

ACHILL ISLAND FISHERY STATISTICS

The table shows the decline in the numbers of basking shark caught off the Irish coast over a 20-year period. Fifty years ago the sight of a large school was commonplace. Now, owing to drastic over-exploitation it is no longer. The basking shark is a protected species around the British coast.

YEAR	NUMBER OF SHARKS TAKEN	TONS (TONNES) OF OIL SOLD
1951	1,630	375 (340)
1953	1,068	230 (209)
1955	1,708	135 (122)
1957	468	104 (94)
1959	280	70 (64)
1961	258	59 (54)
1963	75	19 (17)
1965	47	12 (11)
1967	41	11 (10)
1969	113	29 (26)
1971	29	7 (6)
1973	85	19 (17)
1975	38	9 (8)

PROTECTED SPECIES

After the late 1940's, when basking sharks were killed by harpoons with explosive heads, numbers declined drastically. Basking sharks are slow breeders and though they are now protected, it will be a long time before large numbers build up again.

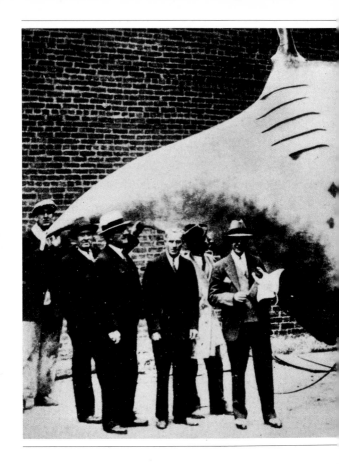

REFERENCE
SECTION

SHARK TALES

SHARKS ARE AMAZING animals but difficult to study, so little is known about them. Many stories are told by sailors, islanders, and fishermen – anyone who encounters a shark usually has a tale to tell. The more we know and understand, the more we can learn to respect such misunderstood creatures.

RARE SPECIES

The megamouth was accidentally discovered in 1976, and only three specimens have since been recorded. Another four specimens reportedly have been found, but have not been officially documented.

MEGAMOUTH

SINKING SHIP

At the end of World War II, *Indianapolis*, the ship that carried part of the Hiroshima atomic bomb, was torpedoed by a Japanese submarine. Of the 883 people who died, most fell victim to sharks, which attacked the survivors for four days until help arrived.

DEADLY TAIL

A sailor is reported to have been decapitated by the tail of a thresher in the Atlantic. Fishermen must be particularly careful of the thresher's powerful tail, since it is almost the same length as its body. The thresher shark is a prized catch. Its spectacular leaps out of the water make it a challenge to land on board.

BIZARRE SHARK

The goblin shark is one of the oddest-looking sharks. It was discovered off the coast of Japan, but was first known from fossil teeth about 100 million years old. The goblin or elfin shark is a deep-water species, colored pink with a brownish tint.

GOBLIN SHARK

GREAT WHITE SHARK

PERSISTENT JAWS

In 1966, a very persistent great white bit the leg of a teenage boy at a surfing beach south of Sydney, Australia. The lifesavers who rescued the boy were stunned to realize that they would have to lift the body of the shark out of the water as well, as it refused to let go. It was not until the shark had been beaten over the head repeatedly that it opened its jaws. Amazingly, the boy's leg was saved.

GOURMET DELIGHT

The poisonous flesh of the greenland shark has a strong taste of ammonia, but is considered a delicacy in Iceland. The flesh is dried for several months before it is eaten. A strong, alcoholic local brew is served with the pieces of shark.

FOLLOW YOUR NOSE

Sharks have a remarkable sense of smell. Lemon sharks, under laboratory conditions, were found to be able to detect the scent of one part tuna fish to 25 million parts seawater. The hungrier the shark, the better its ability to detect the smell of fish in the water.

SLIM CHANCES

In Hawaii, the chance of drowning is more than 1,000 times greater than that of dying from a shark attack. In South Africa, the chance is 600 to 1, and in Australia, it is 50 to 1. However, bees kill more people in Australia each year than sharks do, while more people in the United States are killed by lightning than by sharks.

SOLVING THE PUZZLE

In the 1980's, the US Navy was baffled by disk-shaped bites in the rubber coating of the listening devices on their submarines. By accident, a whale and shark expert was shown the bite marks, which he immediately identified as being those of the little cookiecutter shark.

ANCIENT SHARK

The frilled shark is much the same as sharks that lived 20 million years ago and is the most primitive living species. Its broad-based, pointed teeth are found only in fossil sharks.

The female bears live young, producing 6–12 pups per litter

Snakelike body

Frills on gills

FRILLED SHARK

SHARK RECORDS

EVER SINCE HUMANS first ventured into the water, sharks have fascinated everyone who has encountered them. They come in many shapes and sizes and are indeed remarkable creatures. Scientists are still discovering new information about their biology and behaviour much of which is still unknown.

WHALE OF A FISH

The whale shark is the world's largest fish.The largest scientifically measured specimen was 41.5 ft (12.65 m) long and weighed almost 16.5 to 23 tons (15 to 21 tonnes). It was caught off the coast of Pakistan in 1949. Lengths of over 59 ft (18 m) and weights of 44 tons (40 tonnes) have been reported.

BABY NUMBERS

The gestation period for sharks varies from nine to 22 months. The number of pups born at any one time ranges from one to 100.

OLDER THAN THE DINOSAURS

In terms of animal evolution, sharks are true survivors. They have probably changed less than any other type of vertebrate. One of the oldest fish fossil found so far is a jawless, armored fish called *Arandaspis*, discovered in central Australia. It has been dated to the Ordovician period, almost 500 million years ago.

SMALLEST SIZE

The spined pygmy shark is the world's smallest shark, measuring no more than 10 in (25 cm) long. It lives in deep tropical waters. It has a spine on its first dorsal fin and is luminescent only on its underside, making it hard for predators swimming above to spot.

LONGEST DISTANCE

The blue is the greatest shark traveler. It has been tracked migrating distances of close to 3,726 miles (6,000 km) but mostly travels distances of about 1,550 miles (2,500 km). The mako, tiger, and sandbar sharks are all long-distance swimmers.

BLUE SHARK

FASTEST SWIMMERS

The blue shark and the mako shark are the fastest sharks. When catching food, the blue shark may accelerate to speeds of up to 43 mph (69km/h). It is not possible for sharks to sustain high speeds, and most rarely exceed 7 mph (11 km/h). The fastest fish in the sea is the sailfish which can reach 68 mph (110 km/h).

MOST ABUNDANT SHARK

The piked dogfish is one of the most common species found throughout the world. It is also the most widely eaten species and is fished in large numbers.

GREAT WHITE

MOST DANGEROUS

The great white is responsible for more attacks on humans than any other shark. Hammerheads and tiger sharks are also responsible for many attacks. The sharks that are a threat to people tend to be over 7 ft (2 m) in length. Because of its gruesome reputation, the great white has become endangered, with some countries now declaring it an officially protected species.

JAWS

Peter Benchley's novel *Jaws*, about a killer great white menacing residents of an American vacation resort, is one of the world's best-selling fiction titles. The first Hollywood movie based on the book has become one of the top-grossing films of all time, spawning three sequels, including a 3-D version in which the shark seems to shoot right out of the screen.

This pygmy shark is actual size, and measures only 5 in (13 cm) long

SPINED PYGMY SHARK

CLASSIFICATION

ANIMALS ARE CLASSIFIED into groups that share similar characteristics. Sharks are divided into eight orders. Each order contains families, which include genera and species. Only members of the same species can breed with one another.

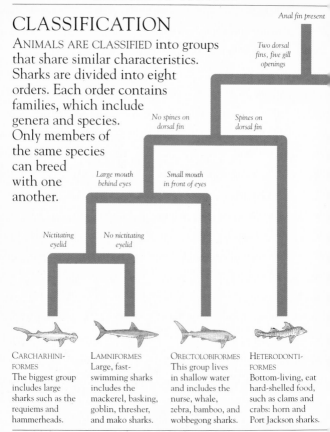

Anal fin present

Two dorsal fins, five gill openings

No spines on dorsal fin

Spines on dorsal fin

Large mouth behind eyes

Small mouth in front of eyes

Nictitating eyelid

No nictitating eyelid

CARCHARHINI-FORMES
The biggest group includes large sharks such as the requiems and hammerheads.

LAMNIFORMES
Large, fast-swimming sharks includes the mackerel, basking, goblin, thresher, and mako sharks.

ORECTOLOBIFORMES
This group lives in shallow water and includes the nurse, whale, zebra, bamboo, and wobbegong sharks.

HETERODONTI-FORMES
Bottom-living, eat hard-shelled food, such as clams and crabs: horn and Port Jackson sharks.

No anal fin present

*One dorsal fin,
six to seven gill
openings*

*Body flattened,
mouth at front*

*Body not
flattened, mouth
underneath*

*Long, sawlike
snout*

*Short snout,
not sawlike*

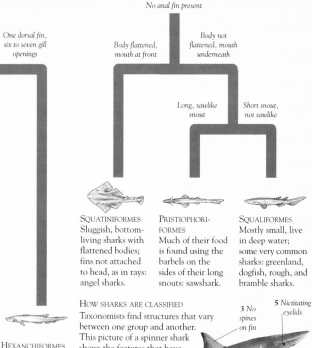

SQUATINIFORMES
Sluggish, bottom-
living sharks with
flattened bodies;
fins not attached
to head, as in rays:
angel sharks.

PRISTIOPHORI-
FORMES
Much of their food
is found using the
barbels on the
sides of their long
snouts: sawshark.

SQUALIFORMES
Mostly small, live
in deep water;
some very common
sharks: greenland,
dogfish, rough, and
bramble sharks.

HOW SHARKS ARE CLASSIFIED
Taxonomists find structures that vary
between one group and another.
This picture of a spinner shark
shows the features that have
been used to construct the
chart on this page.

3 No
spines
on fin

5 Nictitating
eyelids

4 Mouth
behind
eyes

2 Five
gill slits

1 Anal fin present

SPINNER SHARK

HEXANCHIFORMES
Sometimes known
as living fossils; all
have more than
five gill slits: frilled
and cow sharks.

Resources

PLACES WHERE YOU CAN SEE SHARKS

The best place to see sharks in the wild is the tropics. Alternatively, most aquariums have shark exhibits, and some even allow visitors to touch sharks and rays. Here is a sampling of aquariums, all of which have educational and conservation programs as well as viewing tanks or larger displays.

Aquarium for Wildlife Conservation
Surf Avenue and West 8th Street
Brooklyn, New York 11224
The "Sharks Alive" exhibition includes sharks and rays, as well as general information about sharks and their relatives and even cartoons about the lives of sharks.

John G. Shedd Aquarium
1200 South Lake Shore Drive
Chicago, Illinois 60605

Exhibits re-create the natural habitats of leopard, horn, and swell sharks that swim in southern Californian waters, while the Caribbean coral reef hosts nurse sharks.

Monterey Bay Aquarium
886 Cannery Row
Monterey, California 93940
This aquarium has exhibits on the animals that inhabit or visit the bay, and its tank re-creates the aquatic life of the bay.

Mote Marine Laboratory
1600 Ken Thompson Parkway
Sarasota, Florida 34236
The center for Shark Research has an aquarium where sharks of the region are displayed.

National Aquarium in Baltimore
Pier 3
501 East Pratt Street
Baltimore, Maryland 21202

This aquarium has two shark exhibits called "Wings in the Water" and "Open Ocean."

New England Aquarium
Central Wharf
Boston, Massachusetts 02110
In both the Giant Ocean Tank, a re-creation of a coral reef, and smaller tanks, about five shark species are displayed. On the Touch Trolley are samples of shark teeth, sharkskin, and other items for visitors.

Sea World
1720 South Shores Road
San Diego, California 92109
In "Shark Encounter," visitors walk through a tube as they view rays and sharks – brown, lemon, sandtiger, and others.

Sea World
7007 Sea World Drive
Orlando, Florida 32821
The exhibit "Terrors of the Deep" is designed to

instill respect for, not fear of, sharks. Visitors can watch sharks in the "shark theater" or even take a tour behind the tanks and touch a small shark.

Sea World
1100 Southwest Drive
Aurora, Ohio 44202
In "Shark Encounter," visitors walk through a tube as they view rays and sharks – brown, lemon, sandtiger, and others.

Seattle Aquarium
1483 Alaskan Way
Seattle, Washington 98101
Blacktipped sharks swim through a coral reef, while rays can be seen in the underwater dome.

ORGANIZATIONS INTERESTED IN SHARKS

International Union for the Conservation of Nature (ICUN)
Bimini Biological Field Station
University of Miami
9300 Southwest 99th Street
Miami, Florida 33176
Ten regional Shark Specialist Groups responsible to the IUCN cover all tropical seas.

Pelagic Shark Research Foundation
333 Lake Avenue
Santa Cruz Yacht Harbor
Santa Cruz, California 95060
This nonprofit research and educational group works to foster better understanding of sharks.

SOME SHARK PUBLICATIONS

The Life of Sharks
Brudner, Paul. New York: Columbia University Press, 1972

Sharks: Myth and Reality
Caffero, Gaetano, and Maddelena Jahoda. Charlottesville, Va.: Thomasson-Grant, 1994

The Book of Sharks
Ellis, Richard. New York: Knopf, 1989

Sharks: The Perfect Predators
Hall, Howard. Rev. ed. San Luis Obispo, Calif.: Blake, 1993

Shark: Nature's Masterpiece
Lawrence, R. D. Shelburne, Vt.: Chapters, 1994

Natural History of Sharks
Lineaweaver, T. H., III, and R. H. Backus. New York: Lyons and Burford, 1986

Shark
Macquitty, Miranda. New York: Knopf, 1992

World of Sharks
Palmer, Sarah, 6 vols. New York: Random House, 1990

Sharks in Question: The Smithsonian Answer Book
V. G. Springer and J. P. Gold, Washington, D.C.: Smithsonian Institution Press, 1989

Sharks: Silent Hunters of the Deep
Introduction by R. and V. Taylor, New York: DK Publishing, Inc., 1991

Glossary

ADAPTATION
An evolutionary process that enables living things to fit their environment as perfectly as possible. An organ that develops in the uterus of some sharks for the nourishment of the embryo.

AMPULLAE OF LORENZINI
Pores around the snout and head of a shark that contain organs sensitive to weak electric charges in the water.

ANAL FIN
A small fin on the underside of a shark located near its tail.

BARBEL
A sensitive, fingerlike projection near the mouth of some sharks and other fish, which enables them to detect food hidden in mud or sand.

CARTILAGINOUS FISH
Fish that have skeletons formed of cartilage, not bone. They include sharks, skates, rays, chimeras, and banjo fish.

CAUDAL FIN
The tail fin.

CARTILAGE
A firm, gristly material that forms the skeletons of sharks. It is not as hard as bone, though it may be strengthened by calcium salts.

COMMENSAL
An animal that lives in association with a creature of a different species, like a pilot fish with a shark, but each is able to survive without the other.

COPEPOD
One of over 4,500 species of tiny animals – most less than 0.08 inches (2 mm) long – which are an important part of the plankton.

CORNEA
The thick but transparent skin that covers and protects the eyes of animals with backbones and octopuses and squids.

DENTINE
The chief material from which teeth are made.

It is made almost entirely from minerals.

DERMAL DENTICLES
"Skin teeth." These form an armor in a shark's skin. Denticles are made like teeth, with bony bases and an upper part of dentine, covered with enamel. Most dermal denticles have minute ridges, which help guide water over a shark's side so that it swims more efficiently.

DORSAL FIN
A fin on the midline of the back of a fish.

ECOLOGIST
A person who studies the environment.

ENAMEL
The hard covering to the exposed part of a tooth. It is the hardest part of an animal's body.

EMBRYO
A developing animal before it is born or hatched from an egg.

FEEDING FRENZY
The way that sharks compete for food,

regardless of their own safety, when there is blood or abundant food in the water.

FOSSIL
A plant or animal that lived long ago but became preserved in rock after it died.

GALLBLADDER
A small pouch attached to the liver, which stores a substance called bile. Bile has various functions, the most important of which is aiding the digestion of fat.

GESTATION
The period that an embryo takes to develop before birth.

GILL RAKER
A comblike organ growing from a gill arch of a fish, including some sharks. Its function is to strain tiny organisms from the water as it passes over the fish's gills.

GILLS
The breathing organs of fish through which oxygen is taken into the animal's body and waste carbon dioxide is expelled into the water. In sharks and their relatives the gills are unprotected and can be seen as a series of between five and seven slits just behind the head.

INTERNEURALS
Part of the structure of a vertebra of a shark.

LATERAL LINE
A series of pressure-sensitive organs around the head and forming a line down the side of fish.

MIGRATION
Regular movement of an animal population from one area to another and back again, usually on a yearly basis.

NICTITATING MEMBRANE
Often called the third eyelid, the nictitating membrane moves across the surface of the eye to clean and protect it.

OLFACTORY
Concerning the sense of smell.

OVO-VIVIPAROUS
Reproduction where the young develop inside the body but when born, lack a placenta and rely on a yolk sac.

SHAGREEN
The dried skin of a shark. At one time used like sandpaper, for polishing marble and other hard substances.

TAPETUM
A layer of cells that lies behind the retina of some fish and nocturnal animals. It reflects light back into the eye, so that it is used most effectively in dim conditions.

VERTICAL MIGRATION
Movement of marine creatures from one level in the water to another. Many planktonic organisms make vertical migrations daily. They may be followed by fish and other predators.

VIVIPAROUS
Reproduction where the young stays in the mother's body until ready to be born.

Latin name index

A
Angel shark
(*Squatina squatina*)

B
Basking shark
(*Cetorhinus maximus*)
Blackbelly lantern
shark
(*Etmopterus lucifer*)
Blacktip reef shark
(*Carcharhinus
melanopterus*)
Blue shark
(*Prionace glauca*)
Bonnethead shark
(*Sphyrna tiburo*)
Bramble shark
(*Echinorhinus brucus*)
Brownbanded bamboo
shark
(*Chiloscyllium
punctatum*)
Bull shark
(*Carcharhinus leucas*)

C
Caribbean reef shark
(*Carcharhinus perezi*)

Cookiecutter shark
(*Isistius brasiliensis*)

D
Dwarf shark
(*Scyliorhinus torrei*)
Dusky shark
(*Carcharhinus obscurus*)

E
Epaulet shark
(*Hemiscyllium ocellatum*)

F
Frilled shark
(*Chlamydoselachus
anguineus*)

G
Goblin shark
(*Mitsukurina owstoni*)
Great hammerhead
shark
(*Sphyrna mokarran*)
Great white shark
(*Carcharodon
carcharias*)
Green dogfish
(*Etmopterus virens*)

Greenland shark
(*Somniosus
microcephalus*)
Grey reef shark
(*Carcharhinus
amblyrhynchos*)
Gulf catshark
(*Asymbolus vincenti*)
Gulper shark
(*Centrophorus
granulosus*)

H
Horn shark
(*Heterodontus francisci*)
Humantin
(*Oxynotus bruniensis*)

L
Lantern shark
(*Etmopterus sp.*)
Lemon shark
(*Negaprion brevirostris*)
Leopard shark
(*Triakis semifasciata*)
Lesser-spotted dogfish
(*Scyliorhinus caniculus*)
Longnose catshark
(*Apristurus kampae*)

M
Mako shark
(*Isurus oxyrhinchus*)
Manta ray
(*Aetobatus narinari*)
Megamouth
(*Megachasma pelagios*)

N
Nurse shark
(*Ginglymostoma cirratum*)

P
Piked dogfish
(*Squalus acanthias*)
Porbeagle
(*Lamna nasus*)
Prickly dogfish
(Humantin)
(*Oxynotus bruniensis*)
Port Jackson shark
(*Heterodontus portusjacksoni*)

S
Sandtiger shark
(*Eugomphodus taurus*)

Sawfish
(*Pristiophorus cirratus*)
Sawshark
(*Pristiophorus cirratus*)
Seven-gilled shark
(*Notorhynchus cepidianus*)
Silky shark
(*Carcharhinus falciformis*)
Spinner shark
(*Carcharhinus brevipinna*)
Spiny dogfish (piked)
(*Squalus acanthius*)
Spotted wobbegong
(*Orectolobus maculatus*)
Starry ray
(*Raja radiata*)
Starry smoothhound
(*Mustelus asterias*)
Swellshark
(*Cephaloscyllium ventriosum*)

T
Thornback ray
(*Raja clavata*)

Thresher shark
(*Alopias vulpinus*)
Tiger shark
(*Galeocerdo cuvier*)
Tope
(*Galeorhinus galeus*)

V
Varied catshark
(*Parascyllium variolatum*)

W
Whale shark
(*Rhiniodon typus*)
Wobbegong
(*Orectolobus sp.*)

Z
Zebra shark
(*Stegostoma fasciatum*)

Index